ROMAN EGYPT

Classical World Series

Classical World Series

ROMAN EGYPT

Livia Capponi

Bristol Classical Press

First published in 2011 by
Bristol Classical Press
an imprint of
Bloomsbury Academic
Bloomsbury Publishing Plc
36 Soho Square,
London W1D 3QY, UK
&
175 Fifth Avenue,
New York, NY 10010, USA

CIP records for this book are available from the
British Library and the Library of Congress

ISBN 978-1-85399-726-6

Typeset by Ray Davies

www.bloomsburyacademic.com

Contents

List of Illustrations

Preface

Roman Egypt has been my guiding interest for around ten years, since I began writing my dissertation on the transition from Ptolemaic to Roman administration after the provincialisation of Egypt by Augustus in 30 BC. This subject has proved particularly interesting and challenging as it borders several different disciplines, such as papyrology, social and economic history, and the classical languages, Latin and Greek. Mainly for this reason, the study of Roman Egypt has often been confined to a limited number of erudite scholars who could understand the citations and references to papyrological literature and to the texts themselves as a result of their training as classicists and papyrologists. This book aims to present some major topics relating to Roman Egypt in a clear and plain fashion accessible to all students, including those with no previous knowledge of the classical languages and those who, before reading, did not even know what a papyrus was.

My warmest thanks go to my family for supporting me in my work, in particular to my father Mario, who is responsible for the illustrations. Special thanks must go to Megan Trudell, who has checked the English. This book is for my baby son Giovanni, who 'forced' me to write it up before his arrival.

Abbreviations

For the abbreviations of papyri and ostraka I relied on J.D. Sosin, R.S. Bagnall, J. Cowey, M. Depauw, T.G. Wilfong and K.A. Worp (eds), *Checklist of Editions of Greek, Latin, Demotic and Coptic Papyri, Ostraca and Tablets*, available online at the following address: scriptorium.lib.duke.edu/papyrus/texts/clist.html (last updated 11 September 2008).

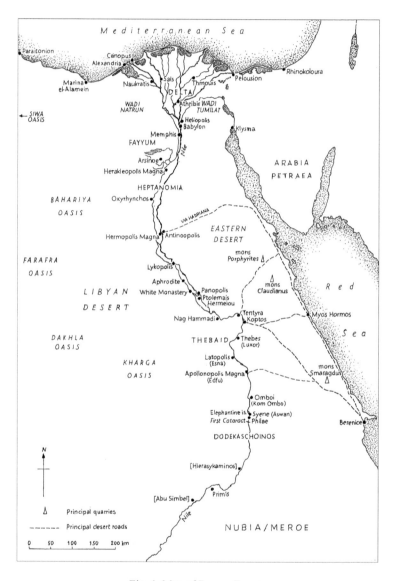

Fig. 1. Map of Roman Egypt.

Chapter 1

The Conquest

Julius Caesar's presence in Ptolemaic Egypt symbolises the importance of the Hellenistic kingdom in the eastern policy of Republican Rome. In 48 BC Caesar landed in Egypt to fight the last part of his war against Pompey. The young son of king Ptolemy XII Auletes, Ptolemy XIII, presented him with the head of the dead Pompey, believing that this would convince Caesar to take his side in his dynastic war against his sister, Cleopatra VII. Caesar, however, was displeased by this dishonourable act and took the side of Cleopatra, with whom he began a love affair. Caesar and the queen had a son named Ptolemy Caesar, unofficially known as Caesarion ('Little Caesar'), who later ruled alongside the queen. After Caesarion's birth, Caesar returned to Rome, leaving his freedman Ruphio and three legions to maintain control of Egypt; we do not know whether his relationship with Cleopatra was 'serious', but it is certainly documented that she visited him in Rome, probably in order to secure benefits for her kingdom.

The death of Caesar on the Ides of March 44 BC was a dangerous blow to Cleopatra and, after the formation of a second triumvirate, the queen met the new Roman leader of the East, Mark Antony. The love story and marriage between Antony and Cleopatra has been recounted hundreds of times, from the age of Plutarch to that of Shakespeare. Following his return from military campaigns in Armenia in 34 BC, Antony granted the conquered territories to the queen at a sumptuous ceremony that explicitly evoked Alexander's empire and conquest of Persia. In the meantime in Rome, Octavian began a war of images and propaganda against Antony, accusing him of having betrayed Roman morals for Hellenistic ambitions of monarchy and of abandoning his Roman wife – Octavian's sister Octavia – for an 'Egyptian whore'. This propaganda helped Octavian to legitimise his war against Antony and Cleopatra which, in reality, aimed at conquering Egypt and securing its huge grain supply. The couple were finally defeated in the naval battle of Actium in 31 BC, and by the time Octavian entered Alexandria in 30 BC they had both committed suicide.

Many Roman soldiers and officials had already settled in Egypt before the formal conquest of 30 BC during the reigns of Ptolemy Auletes and

Cleopatra, as proved by Octavian's Latin edict when he was *triumvir* (43-30 BC) regulating the settlement of some Roman veterans in the Fayum region. Egypt was an extremely rich country and this attracted Roman businessmen and traders. A certain Quintus Ovinius, for instance, is documented as being the chief manager of Cleopatra's textile industries, while a recently published papyrus mentions one Publius Canidius (or Quintus Cascellius, according to a different reading of the text) who was awarded some fiscal privileges by the queen. The document carries a signature which may (according to a recent hypothesis) have been that of Cleopatra in her own hand. This increase in the Roman presence in Egypt probably worried Octavian who revived a Ptolemaic regulation, which stated that nobody should enter or leave Egypt without a passport, possibly out of fear that powerful Romans in Egypt could hijack Rome's corn supply: his targets were, above all, rich Roman senators and prominent knights.

Octavian entered Alexandria on 1 August 30 BC, and all Egypt immediately understood that a new era had begun. On his arrival, Octavian addressed the crowd in Alexandria's hippodrome and demonstrated his clemency by saying that he would spare the city because of its great beauty, its founder Alexander – with whom Octavian evidently identified –, and as a favour to his friend Areius, an Alexandrian philosopher who had taught him in Rome and now accompanied him as a counsellor. Octavian then instituted a cult of himself in the *Kaisareion* of Alexandria – the temple built by Cleopatra and dedicated to Julius Caesar – which was converted into a *Sebasteion* (from *Sebastos*, 'Augustus' in Greek). All temples in Egypt, whether Greek or traditional Egyptian, were obliged to offer daily sacrifices to the emperor. A new city, Nikopolis ('Victory City') was founded near Alexandria on the site of Octavian's military camp, and Greek-style portraits of Augustus were dispatched to the region of Meroe far to the south, so that even the most remote African tribes would know who their new ruler was.

Two days before the formal conquest in 30 BC, Augustus is believed to have ordered the assassination of the sixteen-year-old High Priest of Memphis, a potentially dangerous religious authority, given his wide influence over the Egyptian population, and thus the possible cause of revolts against Rome. Not long after the conquest Augustus imposed a new, invented, era 'of the dominion of Caesar, the son of God' – the god being *divus Julius*, that is Julius Caesar, Octavian's adoptive father. By 30/29 BC the temple lamplighters of Oxyrhynchus were already taking oaths in the name of the new monarch, 'Caesar, God son of God' (*POxy* 12.1453). All Egypt's temples had to worship Octavian along with the

Fig. 2. Coin of Octavian with the legend '*AEGYPTO CAPTA*' ('on the conquest of Egypt').

traditional Egyptian gods, and a high priest of the imperial cult, supervising all the priests and temples of Egypt, was probably introduced in the early years after the conquest.

Octavian's victory at Actium was celebrated and advertised throughout the empire as an epic event that opened the doors to a new golden era characterised by peace – the famous concept of *pax augusta*. Paradoxically, however, Augustus' policy in Egypt in the early years following the conquest was a militaristic one. In the 20s BC Augustus faced local rebellions against the new Roman taxes such as the revolts in the Thebaid, the most turbulent southern region of Egypt, and those in Nubia (modern Sudan); the latter were led by a legendary one-eyed woman, whom the Romans called Candace, the Nubian word for 'queen'. The first Prefect of Egypt, the poet Cornelius Gallus, boasted in a famous inscription on an obelisk now in Rome that he had subdued five cities in the Thebaid in fifteen days. This act of immodesty was regarded to be an offence by Augustus, and Gallus was forced to commit suicide; his name and image were systematically erased from inscriptions and monuments. Yet, at the Roman garrison of Primis (modern Qasr Ibrim) in Lower Nubia, excavators found a papyrus roll of Gallus' verses, perhaps belonging to a Roman soldier garrisoned in the area. Nubia was never really conquered, however, and when the next two Prefects, Aelius Gallus and Publius Petronius, tried to control the region by launching a campaign into Nabatean Arabia, their attempts ended in an inglorious retreat (due, according to their version, to the betrayal of their Arab guide). Naturally, however, we remain ill-informed about these Roman misfortunes, as Octavian kept a firm control over communication and history writing. All we know from the official chronicle of Augustus' achievements, the *Res Gestae*, is that he 'added Egypt to the *imperium* of the Roman people' and then moved, wisely, to a policy of peace.

The institutional, social, fiscal and legal structure imposed by Augustus on Egypt is an exemplary case of how a Hellenistic kingdom could be rapidly turned into a Roman province governed by Roman officials, garrisoned by the Roman army and subject to Roman tributes and law. The striking point is that Augustus' structuring of Egyptian administration and taxes remained more or less unchanged until the third century AD. First, Augustus used Egyptian booty to pay his soldiers. For the same purpose he confiscated all the land and possessions of Cleopatra and Antony and those of their supporters, along with the land belonging to the traditional Egyptian temples which had been the most powerful institutions of the country since Pharaonic times. Former royal land was turned either into 'public land' or into imperial estates – lands with high-revenue crops (e.g. wine and olive oil) and industries (e.g. oil presses or textile works) that Augustus distributed to his relatives, freedmen and friends, so that they would automatically revert to him on the death of the beneficiaries. To improve the production of grain, which was destined to feed Rome, Augustus reorganised the irrigation system of Egypt, the web of canals and dykes that allowed a rainless country to produce over twice as much as a normal harvest by exploiting the annual flood of the Nile. It seems also that the Roman conquest resulted in an increased portion of privately owned land. In particular, the land of the former soldiers of the Ptolemaic army, known as *katoikoi* in Greek, that is colonial settlers, became officially transferable, although it does not seem that a 'free market' existed. As was the case in the Ptolemaic period, most of the land was leased by small-scale farmers who paid rents and taxes to the state. These farmers, once called 'royal farmers', were renamed 'public farmers' in the Augustan period, but their life did not change much for the better. The Roman administration enhanced and developed a system of compulsory services and corvées – called 'liturgies' in the Greek fashion – that partially existed during the Ptolemaic period, so that the wealthiest in the community would take up the most burdensome offices and magistracies and pay for the related expenses out of their own pockets.

This process eventually culminated in AD 202 with the institution of liturgical city councils in every town in Egypt. Compulsory services, corvée labour and taxation were often too heavy a burden for the farmers, who frequently abandoned their homes and disappeared into the desert in order to avoid being registered on official lists and incurring fiscal impositions. This form of strike, called *anachôrêsis*, took place in Egypt from Pharaonic times and continued throughout the Roman period.

Roman prefects of Egypt and their tax officials often exaggerated their requests somewhat, as is vividly documented in a famous reproach from Tiberius to his Prefect of Egypt Aemilius Rectus, probably during an economic crisis caused by excessive taxation: 'I want my sheep to be shorn, not skinned alive!' (Cassius Dio 57.10.5; Suetonius, *Tiberius* 32.2).

The Augustan conquest was greeted as a positive event by traders, who could now access freely the ports of a pacified Mediterranean. Some Alexandrian traders greeted Augustus on the docks of Puteoli, near Naples, as one who allowed them 'to live', echoing, perhaps, an official prayer to Augustus that was recited in the temple for his imperial cult at Alexandria. It is proven that commerce and trade to and from Egypt flourished and business relationships with India, opened by the Ptolemies, increased. The historian and geographer Strabo of Amasia, who went to Egypt around 26-23 BC and included a description of Egypt in his *Geography*, tells us that 'up to a hundred and twenty ships make their way under sail from Myos Hormos for India, whereas previously, under the reign of the Ptolemies, very few people dared to launch their ships and trade in Indian goods' (2.5.12 [118]). Naturally, this information should be used with caution, as Strabo may have wanted to flatter the emperor. Nonetheless there is evidence that Roman senators, bankers and freedmen still invested a lot of money in the Eastern trade. An interesting, yet enigmatic document, the so-called 'Muziris papyrus', registers the entrance into a Red Sea port of a cargo of luxury goods coming from the western coast of India and heading for Alexandria. This ship carried silk, pearls, pepper and other commodities worth almost seven million sesterces, several times more than the minimum fortune of a Roman senator.

A fundamental change introduced by Augustus was the use of the Greek class and Alexandrian citizens as the new governing body of the country, while the Egyptians, as well as other foreign communities present in Egypt, were not integrated into the administration of the empire, unlike citizens of other provinces. Augustus excluded Egyptians from the Roman Senate and even from the army, with the exception of its lowest division, the fleet. Greeks were the only privileged class; they paid reduced taxes and could hope to achieve Alexandrian citizenship, a status necessary in order eventually to obtain Roman citizenship. Space was also reorganised and power was centralised in the capitals (*metropoleis*) of Egypt's regional divisions, specifically in the gymnasia – the educational and recreational centres of the Greek elite. However, the number of Greeks and Alexandrians in Egypt was strictly monitored by the Roman authorities, in an almost racist attempt to preserve the 'purity' of the race. In AD

4/5, Augustus promoted an *epikrisis* or 'scrutiny of the individual status' in the Oxyrhynchite Nome, prescribing that, in order to be one of 'those from the gymnasium', both of an individual's great-grandparents must be from that class. Other documents show that the Greeks of the Arsinoite Nome were also a closed number of 6,475 cavalrymen, their rights and status periodically scrutinised. The Alexandrian citizens, the gymnasial class and the Greek aristocracy were granted fiscal and legal privileges. The most important was the partial or total exemption from the provincial poll tax – called in Egypt *laographia*, 'registration of people', and in other provinces *tributum capitis*, 'tax per head' – introduced soon after the conquest and paid by all adult males aged 14 to 65. As was the case in other provinces, liability for the poll tax (as well as for other taxes and compulsory services) was assessed by a house-to-house census that, at least in Egypt, took place every fourteen years under Tiberius, and possibly every seven years under Augustus.

A Roman knight, the Prefect, took over the place and functions of the old king, while Roman officials with equestrian status took the top posts in the province based in Alexandria, leaving Ptolemaic-style officials to the administration of the nomes (administrative districts) and lesser posts. The *epistratêgoi* supervised groups of nomes while the *stratêgoi* governed the nomes, assisted by local secretaries who were often competent both in Greek and Egyptian. Temple archives and *scriptoria* were replaced by the *grapheion*, the office of the *stratêgos*. In the administration of justice, for example, the chief judge or *archidikastês* continued to supervise tribunals and, although the old tribunal in the royal palace was suppressed, a new tribunal was set up in the gymnasium at Alexandria. Augustus also introduced the yearly *conventus*, an itinerant assize court in which the Prefect and his *consilium*, supported by a newly introduced official, the *iuridicus* or 'dispenser of justice', responded to petitions and adjudicated cases. New archives were created in Alexandria to speed up and centralise the collection and storage of public and private documents and a new legal code was published, the *Gnômon of the Idios Logos*, some copies of which have been preserved from the Antonine period. The extant fragments (*BGU* 5.1210, *POxy* 41.3014) show that Augustan social and moral laws were applied in Egypt, with rigid social and fiscal barriers introduced between Egyptians, Greeks and the Alexandrian elite. Chapters 30 and 32 of the *Gnômon* apply the Augustan marriage laws, prescribing that 'inheritances left to Roman women possessing 50,000 sesterces, if unmarried and childless, are confiscated', and that 'Romans possessing more than 10,000 *sestertii*, if unmarried and childless, do not inherit, but those who have less do inherit'.

Although Augustus radically changed the institutions of Egypt, he often chose to retain Ptolemaic titles and names, perhaps to avoid giving the idea of the imposition of new, foreign rules on a country that traditionally hated foreign masters. For instance, Greek, rather than Latin, was the official language of bureaucracy throughout the Roman period. The consensus until the 1970s was that Egypt was an atypical or peculiar province, set apart from the rest of the empire and governed directly by the emperor. Since then, however, numerous studies have shown beyond doubt that Egypt was not an atypical province (there were no 'typical' provinces) nor a personal possession of the emperor, but a Hellenistic kingdom that was turned into a Roman province, governed by Roman officials and subject to the Roman military, Roman taxation and Roman law. The apparent peculiarity of Egypt rests largely on the peculiarity of our main source of information about it, the papyri. This gigantic and exceptionally detailed body of documents is not found in other provinces; although similar documents exist elsewhere, for instance at Vindolanda on Hadrian's Wall, it is the sheer volume of the Egyptian papyri that is extraordinary. It requires specific technical expertise to decipher and interpret these texts, and this often prevents ancient historians from using them as fully as they ought.

Chapter 2

Forms of Roman Exploitation

Census and poll tax

In the Roman Republican period, various indirect and direct taxes, assessed on different bases and according to different rates, were levied in the provinces. Direct taxes were levied on the entire population while indirect taxes applied only to some goods or services. *Vectigalia* was the technical term for all fiscal revenues from a province, direct and indirect, while *stipendium* was the sum of direct taxes from a province. During the empire, a new categorisation developed: *vectigalia* now indicated only the indirect taxes, while *tributum* denoted the direct taxes imposed on the provinces. *Tributum* in turn could be *capitis* (capitation tax), collected in cash, or *soli* (land tax), collected in kind. In the imperial period the *tributum capitis* was an annual poll tax imposed on all adult males in a province. Every province was supposed to yield a fixed annual sum expressed in cash for the poll tax, however it seems that different provinces, and even different regions within a province, could present different rates. In Roman Asia, apparently, both men and women paid the poll tax while in Egypt it seems that only adult males between the ages of 14 and 62, including slaves, were liable for it. Roman citizens, Alexandrian citizens, some public officials and some categories of priests were totally exempt, along with their slaves, while people of Greek descent paid a reduced rate. The Egyptian population paid the full rate of about 16 to 40 drachmas, probably assessed on the basis of the agricultural productivity of their region.

Some of the money the Roman government extracted from the provinces in the form of tribute was exported, while some remained in the province to pay the Roman troops and the state officials. There were other small direct taxes imposed on provincials, such as the tax for the funding of public baths or taxes on trades, which were collected with the yearly payment of the poll tax. There is documentation of the poll tax until some time in the third century when it was abolished, probably as a consequence of the *Constitutio Antoniniana* (also known as 'Caracalla's Edict') of 212 that conferred Roman citizenship on all citizens of the provinces except the *dediticii* ('rebellious' freedmen who were forever debarred from Roman citizenship).

The introduction of the Roman provincial poll tax was often preceded by a census of the population to assess the number of people liable for it, hence the usage of the term *kensos* to denote the poll tax, e.g. in the Gospels of Matthew (16:25; 17:19) and Mark (12:14). In the Egyptian papyri the term *laographia* ('registration of people') that indicated the census in the Ptolemaic period came to indicate the Roman poll tax from the time of Augustus onwards. The precise beginning of the Roman provincial census in Augustan Egypt is still unknown. Some census declarations seem to show that there were registrations of some categories of population (e.g. public farmers, or priests) as early as 11/10 BC, but it is likely that Augustus took some forms of census soon after the conquest since we know that he did so in other provinces such as Gaul, where he held a general census in 27 BC. Some documents (e.g. *POxy* 4.711) point to an early registration of people before the sixth year of Augustus, around 24 BC. Thereafter, the distribution of tax receipts and declarations suggests that some forms of registration took place around 19/18 BC and 12-10 BC. Other declarations, such as the census declaration of a priest and public farmer from Theadelphia in the Fayum, Harthotes son of Marres, indicate that AD 12 was a census year, while an early declaration of a priest from Oxyrhynchus, Horion son of Petosiris, is probably dated at AD 19. All this evidence has suggested that censuses were taken every seven years up to AD 19; after this date, the census was regularly taken every 14 years – a hypothesis which remains unchallenged. However, it is possible, in my view, that under Augustus there was no such a thing as a provincial census. In other words, Augustus may have taken smaller censuses or registrations of specific categories of the Egyptian population, such as public farmers, or in one region at a time, for instance in the Arsinoite Nome or Fayum first and then in the Thebaid. All that can be stated at present is that during the reign of Tiberius a regular census was taken every 14 years. It is curious that there is also evidence, in the Ptolemaic period, of censuses taken every 14 years. This, in my view, is one more reason to believe that under Augustus different 14-year censuses were taken in different Egyptian districts at different times.

The Roman administration introduced another form of scrutiny of individual status in Egypt: the so-called *epikrisis*, an examination undergone by a limited section of the population who applied for specific fiscal and social privileges such as Alexandrian citizenship or Greek status. In fact, the population of Egypt was divided into clearly demarcated and strictly monitored social classes. Roman citizens (mostly Roman soldiers, veterans, immigrants and freedmen) were the most privileged class, exempt from the poll tax and possessing full legal rights. Alexandrian citizens were also exempt from the poll tax and could apply for Roman citizenship. Then there was the category of 'Greeks', the Hellenised Egyptians that took different names according to their different districts: sometimes they are called 'those from the gymnasium' to indicate their right of entrance into Greek institutions, otherwise they are called the *katoikoi hippeis* (the 'colonial cavalrymen' that used to fight in the Ptolemaic army) or even the *metropolitai*, that is the inhabitants of the district capitals, the *metropoleis*. These 'Greeks' paid a lower rate of poll tax, around twelve drachmas, although there are differences from region to region. Finally, the Egyptians were the lowest in the social hierarchy. They paid the poll tax at the full rate and had no social and legal privileges; they could not enter the Roman army and were excluded from all the institutions of the Greek city, such as the gymnasium.

The case of the Jewish population is more complicated. Many Jews settled in Alexandria in the early Ptolemaic period and attended the gymnasium, so they regarded themselves as Hellenised as Alexandrian citizens exactly like the Greeks. It seems Augustus introduced a more rigid barrier that limited the number of Alexandrians and excluded Jews. This provoked a strong reaction among Alexandrian Jews, who always contested Augustus' measures by arguing that they had been treated exactly like the Alexandrian Greeks in the Ptolemaic period. Echoes of the ancient debate about Alexandria's 'Jewish question' have come down to us through the works of Jews like Philo of Alexandria and Josephus, and it is thus difficult to distinguish the true elements of the story from the apologetic (that is, self-defensive) motifs. There are, in any case, many studies of these problems, most of which reach the conclusion that Jews never enjoyed 'equal citizenship' with the Alexandrians, but were settled in the city as an 'autonomous ethnic community' – the *politeuma* – with independent institutions, cultural centres and magistrates separate from the gymnasium and other Greek institutions in the city.

Augustus may have taken specific registrations for privileged categories (including Egyptian priests) at varying intervals of time, while, as was noted before, the Egyptian population underwent a regular census every 14 years. To what extent the Roman census in Egypt was similar to that which we find in other Roman provinces is hard to say, since every province had its own regional and institutional characteristics. In general, we know little about the ways that censuses were taken in different areas of the empire, and the lack of early Roman or even Ptolemaic census declarations from Egypt does not help. It is possible that much of the registration process was conducted orally through an annual house-to-house inspection (hence the Roman name for the census declarations we

find in Egyptian papyri, *kat' oikian apographê* or 'house-to-house declaration'). Also, the lists of public farmers that were drawn up every year
for the state loan of seed may have been used to create the first census
registers. One must also note that all of the earliest census declarations
come from traditional Egyptian temples: a sign, perhaps, that temples
remained for part of the Augustan period the main centres of literacy and
archival practice, and played a role in the organisation of the early census.

The Roman census often marked the formal annexation of a region as
a Roman province and for this reason was resented (along with the poll
tax) as a symbol of subjugation to Rome and the loss of national independence. Neither the census nor the *epikrisis* was ever popular in Egypt,
where the population reacted by petitioning the prefect, sending delegations to the emperor or openly revolting against Rome. Some fragmentary
documents indicate that an Alexandrian embassy reached Augustus in
Gaul in 10/9 BC and another embassy from the city petitioned the emperor
in AD 12, possibly a census year. A typically Egyptian phenomenon,
documented from the times of the Pharaohs though also present in the
Roman period, is the *anachôrêsis*, or 'flight' from taxes. Often the poorest
villagers simply left their homes, villages and fields and withdrew into
the desert in order to escape census registration and to avoid taxes and
corvées. When tax officials called to conduct the annual house-to-house
inspection, they were informed by the women of the family that the head
of the household had disappeared and left them *aporoi*, 'without substance'. It cannot be a coincidence that the earliest declarations of 'disappearance' belong to AD 19, the earliest confirmed census year under
Tiberius. Jews always fought the imposition of the census (as in AD 6 after
the annexation of Judaea) and animatedly debated whether they should
pay the tribute 'to Caesar' rather than to their real Lord and the Temple
of Jerusalem. A famous echo of this dilemma may be found in the Gospels'
dialogue in which Jesus tells his disciples to 'render unto Caesar that
which is Caesar's' (in this case, Tiberius) and distinguish what they owe
to 'God' (that is, to the Temple of Jerusalem).

Exploitation of the land
At the time of the Roman conquest of Egypt Rome was not yet dependent
on the Egyptian grain supply, but it was clear to Augustus that it was
fundamental to expand the cultivation of soil and improve agricultural
techniques in order to produce more grain for export to Italy. Soon after
the conquest, Augustus had his soldiers dig canals to improve the irrigation system; he confiscated all land belonging to Antony and Cleopatra
and their supporters and created the new category of 'public land'. As in

the Ptolemaic period, most of the land in Egypt belonged to the state and was cultivated by public farmers (called in the Ptolemaic and, in some occasions even in the Augustan period, 'royal farmers') in exchange for both rents and taxes. These farmers received a loan of seed from the state every year, and owed the state a fixed amount of grain calculated on the basis of the productivity and fertility of the land they farmed and the levels of the Nile flood in any particular year. Augustus also introduced the so-called 'imperial estates' – huge properties including land, animals and slaves, that were assigned to members of the imperial *familia*, a broad concept that also included the emperor's friends and slaves. These estates, known as *ousiai* ('substances'), covered the most fertile and productive lands and accordingly provided substantial revenues to the imperial patrimony. On the death of their beneficiary the lands reverted to the emperor, who could reassign them to another friend or relative – for example, the estate of Maecenas reverted to Augustus on the death of the beneficiary. After flourishing during the Julio-Claudian period, the *ousiai* were all confiscated under Vespasian for a specially created branch of the imperial patrimony called the *ousiakos logos*. The Roman emperor and his household retained power over all land and the private account of the emperor or *fiscus* gradually became more important and much richer than the public treasury or *aerarium*, which *de facto* was also controlled by the emperor.

Another major change that Rome brought to Egypt's land system was the official recognition of *katoikic* soldiers' land as private land, and the expansion of all land in private hands. Often the Roman state sold off dry or unproductive land to private citizens who then put the land back into cultivation by investing their own private capital. This strategy had existed in Ptolemaic times, but was probably enhanced in the Roman period. Traditional Egyptian temples also lost much of their land, which was confiscated and became public, although they often leased it back from the Roman state and continued to cultivate it in exchange for rent. Tax rates on the land remained pretty stable throughout the first two centuries of Roman rule: while the land of the *katoikoi* generated a low tax of one *artaba* (the measure of grain) per *aroura* (the measure of land) – approximately one tenth of the annual grain produce – the estates and private land were liable for higher taxes that amounted to as much as five or six *artabas* per *aroura*, that is one quarter or one third of total produce.

Other taxes

Among the direct taxes, the most important apart from the poll tax was the *chômatikon*, or 'dyke tax' at an annual rate of 6 drachmas and 4 obols. From the reign of Augustus onwards, this tax was levied on all Egyptian males including priests and contributed to the organisation of the web of canals and dykes that formed the only irrigation system possible in such a dry country. Irrigation had a direct impact on grain revenue, thus the cleaning and digging of canals and the construction of dykes to direct the Nile flood constituted a crucial issue for Egypt's economy. The *chômatikon* was often collected together with the poll tax and other direct taxes and, for those who could not pay, either Augustus or one of his successors introduced a new corvée called *penthêmeros*, 'five days' – named for the number of days of forced labour on the canals it entailed. Augustus also introduced a new levy called 'impost on behalf of the poor', a surtax of 4 to 7 drachmas per year imposed on the whole population that was intended to compensate for taxes not paid by those with no income. While both the dyke tax and the tax on behalf of the poor seem to have been introduced by Augustus, the tax called *arithmêtikon katoikôn*, that is 'for the enumeration of the *katoikic* soldiers' was probably inherited from the Ptolemaic period. This tax (the rate of which seems to have varied from 16 to 28 drachmas per year, perhaps according to the size of the holding) was collected from every owner of *katoikic* land, that is the land of the military settlers. It may have served as a tax on the ownership of this privileged category of land, or as a way of keeping an accurate record of all the *katoikoi* who were settled on the land. A precedent for this tax called the 'capitation tax of the *katoikoi*' is documented in the Ptolemaic period. In general, a comparison with the taxation system of Persian Egypt shows that the taxes, as well as the weights and measures, adopted in Roman Egypt had Persian precedents.

The Roman state took over the proto-industries and monopolies established by the Ptolemaic kings, such as access to the public baths and the production of beer and oils and papyrus: the respective taxes were thus directed to the imperial patrimony, the *fiscus*. Public baths were established during the Ptolemaic period for the use of the Greek élite, and were often located near gymnasia. In the Roman period this system was maintained and two types of taxes were levied: one tax of approximately 7 drachmas 5 obols was imposed on some (though probably not all) people around a specific bath as a contribution to its maintenance, while a separate rent or an entrance fee could be paid to lease the bath or simply to access it, exactly as our taxes fund public swimming pools today, yet we still pay a small fee to use them. Another former monopoly of the Ptolemies was the beer industry. Breweries belonged to the king but could be leased by private companies, and were often located in traditional Egyptian temples which paid a licence fee to the state. In the Roman period, beer brewers seem to have paid a state tax called *zytêra* or 'beer tax' that was imposed at individual rates on each beer producer and probably varied according to the amount of beer consumed in the brewery. The Roman administration also took over the most important of Ptolemaic monopolies, the production and commerce of oils, especially sesame and other seed oils, that were used both as nutrients and for lighting. In Roman Egypt an 'oil tax' or *elaikê* was levied in the Augustan period too, although the evidence for it is scanty. It is likely that taxes and rents were exacted from those who leased state-owned oil presses. During the Roman period these facilities were often on imperial estate land, owned directly by the imperial family: the oil press on the estate of the freedman Narcissus, for instance, paid a fee of 200 drachmas (probably per month) – a sign that it was an important industrial complex. Finally, from the Ptolemaic period onwards, a tax called *chartêra* was raised on papyrus. It was probably a licence to sell or manufacture papyrus, or else a fee on the revenues of the papyrus industry. In the Roman period it seems that, once again, papyrus marshes were often part of the imperial *patrimonium* so that all these taxes were seized directly for the private patrimony of the emperor and his family. In one lease of a papyrus marsh from 14/13 BC (*BGU* 4.1180) the lessees acknowledge the receipt of a loan of 200 drachmas which they promise to return in instalments along with portions of the harvest over six months. These 200 drachmas were probably equal to the rent for one (or more) months which the lessees were not able to pay. Augustus also continued to impose trade taxes or *cheironaxia*, such as the tax on weavers or *gerdiakon* at the rate of approximately 28 drachmas per year, which were often collected together in one payment with the poll tax; the weaving industry itself came under the control of Roman managers.

Among the indirect taxes, the most important was the sales tax or *enkyklion*, a contribution of varying amounts paid as a percentage (that is, *ad valorem*) of around 5 to 10 percent on market sales, donations, mortgages and the manumission of slaves. The collection of this tax was delegated to publicans or tax farmers, who worked in the city or village market together with the *agoranomos* or supervisor of markets. Many documents also mention taxes on animals, for instance a tax on the grazing rights of sheep and goats (called *ennomion*, 'pasture tax', which was levied on the basis of the annual declaration of ownership of these animals submitted at the beginning of the year throughout Egypt. This tax served, like its Roman equivalent the *scriptura*, to keep control of the number of privately owned animals pastured on state land. There was also a tax of 5 drachmas on the ownership of donkeys, the most important means of transport in Egypt, and a tax on pigs, another property tax assessed on the basis of declarations of pig ownership. The taxes on temples and priests were continued without significant change from the Ptolemaic period. Tax rates were also quite stable throughout the Roman period until the end of the second century AD.

Tax collection
A large and continually increasing number of tax receipts and tax registers preserved on Egyptian papyri and ostraca provide a fresh and reliable body of evidence that enlightens us about the criteria and dynamics of Roman fiscal practice in Egypt. It is likely that Augustus took much of the essential structure of his taxation system from Ptolemaic Egypt, although the comparison is hindered by the lack of Ptolemaic evidence and by the irregular distribution (in both time and space) of the extant tax receipts. What we can say is that taxes were assessed every year through a sophisticated system of records and accounting that probably inherited and extended the main lines of the Ptolemaic system. District officials, for example the *stratêgos,* submitted an annual estimate of the revenue available and, on this basis, the prefect in Alexandria established the entire amount of taxes that should be extracted from the province, probably by issuing a *gnômon* or 'tax schedule'. The main novelty under Roman rule was that the emperor controlled all the empire's revenue and dictated the amount of taxes to be extracted from every province. The prefects had thus to answer directly to the emperor and could be punished for extracting too little or even too much from their provinces.

It is often difficult, if not impossible, to judge whether taxation was uniform throughout the province, but it is likely that taxes were imposed at different levels according to each region's agricultural productivity. Scholars have argued that the Roman conquest brought about a substantial change in the method of collection of taxes: while in the Ptolemaic period the collection of taxes was carried out by partnerships of *telônai* (the equivalent of the Latin *publicani*) who bought the right to levy the royal dues for a percentage of the revenues, that is they were contracted to pay a lump sum, during the Roman period, possibly from the time of Augustus, taxes were levied by state officials whose work was a compulsory service, while *publicani* were used to levy indirect taxes only. In other words, in Roman Egypt as well as in other Roman provinces direct taxes (e.g. the poll tax) were collected by state-appointed officials called *praktores*, while *telônai* or tax farmers, selected from the wealthiest of the villages or the *metrôpoleis*, were confined to the levy of indirect taxes (e.g. the sales tax). For Rostovtzeff, the office of tax collector might have been 'liturgical' (a compulsory service imposed on the richest members of the community) from the late Ptolemaic period, as people tended to avoid the office since they could not hope to make enough profit from it and would often have to pay with their own money for any deficit or tax evasion on the part of any member of their community. There might have been a Hellenistic precedent for the Roman system of compulsory services in Egypt, although this cannot be definitely proven. It is also likely that Roman companies of *publicani* which we see in other provinces never set foot in Egypt; this was probably for linguistic reasons, since a knowledge of both Greek and Egyptian was required in order to collect taxes from the local communities. Therefore, Roman officials, including the freedmen and slaves of the emperor, probably limited themselves to controlling the revenue presented to the state treasuries in Alexandria.

There was a clear change following the Roman conquest regarding the collection of grain revenue, the most important element of both the Egyptian and the Roman economies. During the Ptolemaic period the chief officials in the collection of the grain tax were the *sitologoi* – state officials who worked at the state granaries in every village and in the nome capitals, and issued the annual distribution of seed grain to the royal farmers; the village officials, such as the *kômogrammateus* ('village secretary') and the *topogrammateus*, participated in the operation by confirming that the farmers who received the seed were actually farming the said amount of land. In the Augustan period, the former royal granaries were made public and the role of *sitologoi* possibly became a compulsory service. In addition, officials called *phorologoi* supervised the collection of the grain tax and the distribution of seed from the *sitologoi* to the public farmers. These supervising officials are documented in the Augustan period only, and were often freedmen or slaves of the emperor from Italy with their own staff of subordinate slaves called *vicarii, actores* or *vilici.* These imperial figures resided in Alexandria but supervised the local, Egyptian-speaking, tax collectors throughout Egypt. This system is a clear indication of the strict and direct control that the imperial family exercised over the revenues of the province. Under Tiberius or Claudius, imperial freedmen and slaves were probably gradually replaced by imperial procurators of equestrian rank.

In Roman Egypt tax collectors underwrote with their own private fortune potential deficits in the amount of revenues collected. The village community, too, was often held responsible for any of its members' financial shortfall and had to supply payment on behalf of those who could not pay (according to the principle, present from the Ptolemaic period, of the 'collective responsibility for deficits' that derived from Greek law). Some passages in Philo vividly describe the tortures and abuses that tax collectors underwent in the Roman period. Tortures such as the rack were commonly inflicted on either taxpayers or, more often, tax collectors who failed to submit the agreed lump sums, and the *praktoreion* or public prison was mainly used to detain tax evaders and debtors. Another passage in Philo informs us that in cases of tax default, Egyptians were whipped while Alexandrian citizens could be beaten with flat (and therefore less painful) implements, as a special privilege. Philo's description of the abuses that accompanied tax collection in the Julio-Claudian period has been confirmed by recently published documents; his accounts must therefore be less exaggerated than modern scholarship has often assumed.

Coinage and monetary circulation

Coinage acquired a special power under Augustus when it began to reach all social classes from the urban Hellenised elites down to the Egyptian village farmers. Excavations show that the coinage in use in Roman Alexandria, the *tetradrachm*, was by far the largest provincial silver currency. Augustus introduce a wide number of smaller denominations and designs that are unparalleled both in the Ptolemaic period and under subsequent Roman emperors.

Roman Egypt was vital to the rest of the empire not only for its grain, but also for its outflow of money in the form of taxation. However, Egypt had a closed currency system, which meant that Egyptian coinage could not be exported outside the province. As recent studies have shown, the majority of financial transactions took place through credit and letters of exchange. Often imperial freedmen and slaves or the imperial procurators with their huge bank accounts served as guarantors for the export of cash from Alexandria to Italy. Traders also played an important role in making markets more dynamic. It is likely, however, that most transactions between the imperial government and the provinces (not only Egypt) were made in the form of bills of exchange in banks. Egyptian evidence thus shows that Roman finance was more sophisticated than has often been assumed.

Chapter 3

Roman Emperors in Egypt

The view of Rome from Alexandria

Alexandria and Egypt were at the centre of Mediterranean politics in the Roman period. The most important symbol and tourist attraction at Alexandria was the mummy of Alexander the Great which was buried in a transparent coffin allegedly made of glass (more probably of alabaster) and preserved in the Mausoleum, probably close to the tombs of the Ptolemaic kings. Throughout the Roman imperial period the body of Alexander symbolised the idea of absolute monarchy and universal empire and, for this reason, was an object of admiration and attraction for all Roman leaders who wished to present themselves as world conquerors like Alexander. Julius Caesar was the first to visit the tomb of Alexander, and Augustus and other emperors after him did the same. After Augustus not many emperors bothered to go and visit Egypt, but most of those who made the journey did so for strategic reasons: throughout the Roman period to arrive at Alexandria as a victorious general and to conquer the rebellious, independent-minded Alexandrian crowd – above all, to control the granaries which supplied Rome with corn – meant to have the world in your hands.

Germanicus, a nephew of Augustus, went to Egypt in AD 19 to see the antiquities of the region, according to Tacitus. In reality, the young prince was sent by the emperor Tiberius as an imperial representative in the Near East to make alliances and hold diplomatic meetings with the kings and dynasts of Armenia and Parthia. However, economic crisis and famine in Egypt made Germanicus' presence necessary. The prince became popular in Alexandria because he opened some state granaries and lowered the price of corn. He also passed some edicts regulating prices and requisitions in order to help the suffering Alexandrian population. His predilection for Greek habits and clothes (which Roman authors found disgraceful) endeared him to Alexandria's Greek nobility. A document on papyrus (*POxy* 25.2435 *recto*) describes in vivid detail one of his appearances at the hippodrome where an excited crowd applauded him and enthusiastically proclaimed him a god. Another document shows that Germanicus passed a specific edict that refused divine honours in order not to offend Tiberius (*SB* 1.3924, *SelPap* 2.211). According to Tacitus, Tiberius, jealous of Germanicus' popularity and fearing that he could lay claim to the imperial throne from Alexandria, ordered him to leave the country and possibly later ordered his death by poisoning. Tiberius also reduced the number of legions garrisoning Egypt from three to two, probably to prevent insurrections: he was already aware of 'a secret of the empire' (the *arcanum imperii* mentioned by Tacitus, *Histories* 1.4) that would be realised only a few decades later – i.e. that the Roman emperor could be elected outside Rome – and Alexandria seemed to be the ideal place for such 'alternative' imperial elections.

Caligula visited Alexandria and, according to ancient gossip, removed the cuirass from Alexander the Great's mummy and wore it himself in megalomaniacal fashion. Neither Claudius nor Nero bothered to visit Egypt, although in AD 61 Claudius sponsored an exploration of southern Egypt and Ethiopia. Nero, by contrast, had planned a trip to Alexandria and had ordered his friend Caecina Tuscus, the prefect of Egypt, to build a new residence and expensive baths for his future visit. Unfortunately, the prefect dared to use the baths that had been built for the expected visit and was banished. Nero's Philhellenism probably extended to the population of Alexandria, and to Egypt's Greek cities. A papyrus letter of Nero's addresses a delegation from the capital of the Fayum, Ptolemais Euergetis, that in turn may have been connected with an official selection of the Greek élites in Egypt. It is likely that Nero's policies, like those of Augustus, created rigid legal and fiscal barriers between the class of Alexandrians and some privileged Greeks (especially the descendents of Greek soldiers, or the gymnasial class) and the rest of the Graeco-Egyptian population. Throughout the Roman period the Alexandrians and some closed groups of Greek soldiers were the only real élite in Egypt, while the Egyptian population lived in very poor conditions, under a heavy fiscal burden. For the first two centuries of Roman rule no Egyptian could enter the Roman senate, and Augustus had decreed that no Egyptian could enter the Roman army, so that they would not be eligible for the Roman citizenship that was granted on discharge from service.

In AD 69, the so-called 'year of the four emperors', a prophecy circulated throughout the Near East that 'a man from Palestine would become the ruler of the world'. The prophecy came true when the general Vespasian, who was fighting against the Jews in Judaea, was proclaimed emperor by his troops on 1 July 69 in Alexandria – with a little help from the prefect of Egypt, Tiberius Julius Alexander. An extract from an official chronicle on papyrus (*PFouad* 8; *CPJ* 2.418a) reports that, in an overcrowded hippodrome, the Alexandrians greeted their new emperor as 'saviour and benefactor' – the same titles that characterised the Ptolemaic kings – and also as 'Son of Ammon' and 'Rising Sun', the titles of the Egyptian pharaohs. Some Roman literary sources (Cassius Dio 65.8; Suetonius, *Vespasian* 19.2), however, claim that the Alexandrians insulted and ridiculed him. Apparently, Vespasian had blockaded the grain supply from Egypt to Rome in order to blackmail the senate and obtain ratification of his election to the imperial throne; it is thus possible that some Roman sources were initially hostile to him. Vespasian's son Titus entered Alexandria after the conquest of Jerusalem (Suetonius, *Titus* 5, Josephus, *Bellum Judaicum* 7.116); a private letter (*POxy* 34.2725) offers a precise date for the occasion: 'the lord Caesar entered the city on 25 April 71 at seven in the morning'. After the fall of the last rebellious fortress of Masada by the Dead Sea in 73 the numerous Jewish community of Cyrene joined the Jewish rebellion against Rome. Vespasian rushed to North Africa and ordered that the Jewish temple of Leontopolis near Heliopolis in Egypt be closed and razed to the ground, for fear that it could became the focus of the revolution.

In the period between 116 and 117 Egypt was again at the centre of Roman imperial politics. The local Jewish communities revolted against both the Alexandrian Greeks and Rome, and the region of Cyrenaica was also at the centre of the revolt. The Jews elected leaders and marched eastwards to 'liberate' the Eastern world from the Roman occupation; recent studies show that the so-called Diaspora revolt of 116-117 seriously challenged the stability of the Roman empire, and both Trajan and the future emperor Hadrian were involved in repressing the uprising.

Literary sources such as the historian Appian of Alexandria, an Egyptian contemporary (Appian, *Arabicus Liber* fr. 19; *Bella Civilia* 2.90), tell us the story of the revolt from the point of view of the winners, describing Jews as bloodthirsty barbarians who represented a threat to the civilised West. The documentary papyri are particularly interesting testimonies to the consequences of the war that eventually brought about the virtual obliteration of all Jewish communities in Egypt. These were also written by Greeks or Roman soldiers and are profoundly anti-Jewish. In a series of documents from the office of Apollonios, the *stratêgos* of the Apollonopolite Nome, we find interesting references to the disasters of the war. Eudaimonis, the mother of the *stratêgos*, talks about damage to the fields and villages, the consequences for trade and the lack of food supplies that made her life difficult, and she threatens the gods that she will pay no attention to religion 'until I get my son back safe' (*CPJ* 2.438 and 442). When the revolt was repressed, Egypt's Greeks instituted a festival to commemorate the event, which continued to be celebrated annually for more than 80 years (*CPJ* 2.450). The archive of papyrus letters from the soldier Claudius Terentianus, enrolled in the Roman army in Egypt, to his friend and patron Claudius Tiberianus, a Roman veteran settled in Karanis (Fayum), discuss the Diaspora revolt in terms of civil strife in Alexandria. Terentianus was actually wounded in the war and Tiberianus, although he had resigned active military service (or was about to do so) around 116, continued his career as an agent of the provincial governor's intelligence service.

Hadrian and the Antonines
When Trajan died on 8 August 117 Hadrian was in Antioch, and was soon proclaimed emperor. On 25 August the new prefect of Egypt, Rammius Martialis, sent out a circular letter, preserved on papyrus (*POxy* 55.3781), officially informing the Egyptian *stratêgoi* of Hadrian's accession and instructing them to declare festivities in their districts: 'therefore we shall pray to the gods that his continuance may be preserved to us for ever and shall wear garlands for ten days', while a temple account from Soknopaiou Nesos (*StudPal* 22.183) lists provisions and expenses for the celebration of a festival to Hadrian called 'Hadrian's days'. In *PGissLit* 4.4, a fragment of a dramatic performance specially composed and performed at Apollonopolis Heptacomia (Kom Isfaht) in the Thebaid to mark Hadrian's accession, the god Apollo declares: 'Having just mounted aloft with Trajan in my chariot of white horses, I come to you people … to proclaim the new ruler Hadrian, whom all things serve on account of his virtue and the genius of his divine father'. The people: 'Let us make merry, let us kindle our hearts in sacrifice, let us surrender our souls to laughter'.

Both the literary sources and the documents suggest that, in August or early September 117, Hadrian went to Judaea and made the region a *provincia consularis*, appointing a new governor, Lucius Cossonius, and ordering that Jerusalem be renamed *Aelia* in his name (Aelius Hadrianus). Thereafter, in September or October 117, the new emperor probably visited Alexandria. Documents referring to Hadrian's edicts and benefactions in favour of the Egyptian farmers and other categories of the local population can be explained only by hypothesising that Hadrian was present in Egypt in 117. Egypt's agricultural produce was of great importance to Rome and, in addition, control over this crucial province was essential to ensure the survival of the new emperor since his position was not secure and his sudden change of policy from that of his predecessor placed him in danger.

By visiting Alexandria, a city that had always represented the potential alternative capital of the Roman empire and a place where any charismatic general could hope to become emperor, perhaps Hadrian aimed to legitimise his accession to the imperial throne. Vespasian, as has been said above, had entered Alexandria after subduing the Jewish revolt in 70, and was proclaimed emperor there. In Alexandria, Hadrian played the role of world benefactor and bringer of peace and religious freedom. He restored temples and buildings destroyed in the Jewish revolt, built temples in the traditional Egyptian style – as had Augustus and other emperors before him – and opened new temples that worshipped Greek and Roman gods together with the imperial gods of Victory and Fortune. Back in Rome in 118, Hadrian started building his magnificent villa at Tibur (Tivoli), where Egyptian images and motifs play a major role. He even reconstructed some historical Alexandrian monuments, such as the Canopus or gymnasium, on a smaller scale in his garden.

In 129-130 Hadrian visited Egypt again. He witnessed the installation of the Apis bull in Memphis, hunted lions in the desert and visited the main cities during a Nile cruise. The chronicles of Hadrian's voyage on the Nile, including Marguerite Yourcenar's famous *Memoirs of Hadrian*, are all overshadowed by one main event: the death of beautiful Antinous, the emperor's lover, who drowned in the river on 22 October 130 under mysterious circumstances. It was rumoured that his death had been a voluntary, 'religious', sacrifice aimed at saving the reputation of the emperor. Next to the site of the incident, Hadrian founded a Greek city called Antinoupolis, a Roman *colonia* with privileged fiscal and legal status that was modelled on the Athenian system of tribes and assemblies. According to Egyptian tradition, anyone who drowned in the sacred river had special divine blessing and Hadrian soon instituted a cult of Antinous, which rapidly spread throughout the Greek-speaking part of the empire. Hadrian probably favoured this cult in order to cement the loyalty of subject communities to Rome. Hadrian also initiated the building of a Red Sea coastal road known as *Via Hadriana*.

In 153, under Hadrian's son Antoninus, new riots broke out in Alexandria in which Prefect Lucius Munatius Felix was killed, and an epidemic known as the 'Antonine plague' – probably smallpox – caused a major decline in population in the period from 167 through the 170s. Under Marcus Aurelius in 172 there was a major insurrection, the so-called revolt of the *boukoloi* (literally 'herdsmen'), led by the Egyptian priest Isidoros. The *boukoloi* were political groups of lower-class desperadoes who fought against the Roman forces and Roman religion in defence of Egyptian political and religious independence. Western sources depict these people as fanatics and even transvestites and cannibals. Apparently the *boukoloi*, disguised in female clothing, approached a centurion pretending to offer gifts and, after killing him, sacrificed the body, pledged an oath on his entrails and then ate them as part of a strange demonic communion. Isidoros defeated the Romans in battle and had almost conquered Alexandria when Avidius Cassius, governor of Syria and the son of a Prefect of Egypt, strategically divided the rebels and managed to defeat them after several battles. (Dio [Xifilinus] 71.4; *Historia Augusta: M. Ant.* 21.2; *Avid. Cass.* 6.7). However, the story has a surprise ending: in 175, Avidius Cassius travelled from Syria to Alexandria and obliged his troops to declare him emperor. A fragmentary document (*SB* 10.10295), possibly a report made by the president of the council of Antinoupolis on his return from Alexandria on the accession of Avidius Cassius, preserves part of a letter in which Cassius states it is his right to be elected emperor because he was born in Alexandria when his father was Prefect of Egypt. Two centuries after the suicide of Antony and Cleopatra, in AD 175, the revolt of Avidius Cassius disclosed another 'secret': that the empire could be divided into Eastern and Western sub-empires, with Alexandria as the potential capital of the East.

Marcus Aurelius spent the winter of 176 in Alexandria and eventually quelled the sedition, punishing and confiscating the property of all who had allegedly helped Avidius Cassius during his three-month rule. Among the victims of such confiscations and persecutions were many Christians, who were accused of political sedition against Rome. When, a few years later, Marcus Aurelius and his son Commodus travelled in the East, they were addressed in numerous speeches, orations and works by Christian bishops and writers – the so-called apologists – who strenuously defended Christianity from the accusation and struggled to prove that Christians throughout the empire were utterly loyal to the emperor and even contributed to the growth and defence of the Roman empire. Some examples include Apollinaris, who recalled episodes in which Christian soldiers remained loyal to Marcus Aurelius on the Danube in 175, and Melito, bishop of Sardis, who protested against Roman decrees that ordered the expropriation of Christian property and the persecution of Christians and asserted the loyalty of Christians to the empire. In 177, Athenagoras said that no slave would accuse the Christians, even falsely, of murder or cannibalism and, in 180 or 181, Theophilus, bishop of Antioch (*To Autolycus* 1.11) stressed Christian loyalty to the emperor. Two decades later, Tertullian still spoke of the loyalty of Christian soldiers to Marcus Aurelius and reiterated that no Christians had supported Cassius. All of these apologetic works may well have reflected laws passed in 176-180 that punished Christians and confiscated their property as retribution for their supposed participation in the revolt of Avidius Cassius. We do not know to what extent these speeches mirrored reality.

The Severans

Following some problems with the imperial succession and a series of short-lived emperors, Septimius Severus became emperor in 193. Originally from North Africa, Severus was the first emperor to allow Egyptians to enter the Roman Senate, a revolutionary move that finally removed the stigma of inferiority and barbarity that Augustus had imposed on the Egyptians. Severus visited Alexandria around 200-202 and the policies he introduced there represent an important turning point in the administration of the country. Severus' reforms are preserved on a large papyrus roll containing 31 brief *apokrimata*, or 'imperial rescripts'. The most important change was that which modern scholars call 'municipalisation' – the introduction of city councils or *boulai*, the Greek equivalent of Roman municipal senates, both in Alexandria and in the capitals of the Egyptian districts that became equivalent to Roman *municipia*. Under municipalisation, the cities were governed by an assembly of magistrates selected on the basis of their wealth who paid an entrance fee and wore crowns of office. The councillors were also responsible for the collection of taxes. These measures were aimed at tackling the country's serious economic crisis and, apparently, attempted to favour Egyptian farmers. In fact, one document (*PCattaoui* 2; *SB* 1.4284) shows some Egyptian farmers recalling the visit of Severus and his son Caracalla in admiring terms: 'When the most sacred emperors ... arose like the sun in Egypt'. Severus was less open-minded with regard to religion. Fearing, perhaps, the increasing power of Christians in Egypt, he suppressed the influential Christian School of Alexandria and outlawed conversion (Clement, *Stromateis* 2.20; Eusebius, *Historia Ecclesiastica* 5.26; 6.1). A large number of Christians preferred to die rather than forsake their religion. The ideology of martyrdom, which the Christians had inherited from Judaism, characterised the relationship between Rome and Christianity throughout the third century.

Severus' son Caracalla is remembered above all for his *Constitutio Antoniniana* of 212, an edict that extended Roman citizenship to the empire's entire male adult population, excluding *peregrini dediticii*, rebellious freedmen forever debarred from Roman citizenship. This provision, part of which is preserved on papyrus (*PGiss* 40), may have been issued in order to extend the inheritance tax and other taxes imposed on Roman citizens to all of the empire's inhabitants in order to alleviate the economic crisis, and probably appeared less important to contemporaries that it does to us. The mass bestowal of Roman citizenship on the inhabitants of Egypt is signalled clearly in the papyri by the sudden and ubiquitous insertion of the name *Aurelius* (Caracalla's own name) before the proper name (Greek or Egyptian) of any inhabitant. Documents show that in 215 Caracalla visited Alexandria, but the event was disastrous for the city since the emperor quelled a demonstration, expelled Egyptian natives from the city, closed the theatres and suppressed the so-called *syssitia*, the dining rights of scholars at the Museum, in a counter-reformation that marked the beginning of the cultural and political decline of Alexandria. The last emperor of the Severan dynasty, Severus Alexander (222-235), visited Egypt – or at least planned to do so, a papyrus document informs us – in order to halt the country's excessive fiscal and liturgical impositions on Rome.

The third-century crisis
In spite of the Severan reforms and the establishment of the new council-based system in Egypt, the third century was characterised by a profound economic crisis which was aggravated by the imperial government's financial crisis. Since the time of Augustus, Egypt and its grain produce had been used to save the empire from financial problems, but now the country did not have the resources to satisfy both internal and external demands. New taxation was resisted, the liturgical system vacillated and the population declined. The conflict between tax collectors and the population was violent, and failure to collect and deliver all due taxes could lead to trial, fines and the confiscation of one's property by the treasury – hence the widespread social discontent which caused revolt in the villages.

The crisis also affected the middle class and the once privileged categories: in a document from Oxyrhynchus from AD 260 (*PCollYoutie* 60), a teacher complains that his salary, when he is fortunate enough to get it, is paid in sour wine and grain that has been eaten by worms, and he asks for a small plot of land in order to be able to continue in his job. Paradoxically, however, archaeological excavations seem to point to a third-century boom in Roman-style civic buildings such as porticoes, processional areas, gymnasia, baths and theatres. One explanation for this apparent contradiction is that public works were an area in which the councils were autonomous and civic pride may also have played a role.

An attempt at reform was made by Philip the Arab (244-9): in a papyrus document his procurators claimed to be 'lightening the burden of all Egyptians, worn down as they are by the limitless liturgies' (*POxy* 33.2664). However, Philip's reforms were double-edged and, it seems, actually planned to increase imperial revenues. For this reason, therefore, they did not solve the problem. One bad sign for the administration of

Egypt is that the census returns cease after 257/8 and no censuses were taken after the third century. After the failure of Philip's reforms, the emperors Aurelian (270-275) and Probus (276-282) made new efforts. Aurelian hoped to revive agriculture throughout the empire by reorganising Nile transport and Probus worked on the system of dykes and canals, but the crisis persisted (*Historia Augusta: Aurelian* 47). In 270-272 Aurelian fought the caravan city of Palmyra and its formidable queen Zenobia who had occupied Egypt, and in 273 Aurelian had the Museum razed to the ground to punish the Alexandrians for a revolt; scholars either fled the country or sought refuge in the smaller library of the temple of Serapis or Serapeum. Once again, the cultural and political aspirations of Alexandria had been frustrated. The military prevailed and the decline of Egypt as a key area of the Mediterranean put an end to Alexandria's dreams of finding glory as the 'capital of the East'.

Chapter 4

Byzantine Egypt and the End of Roman Rule

In 284 the emperor Diocletian (284-305) instituted a comprehensive reform. He divided the empire into eastern and western halves and Egypt itself into smaller provinces in order to increase administrative efficiency. Egypt was also forced to give up its closed currency system and its unique calendar; it was integrated into the systems in use across the rest of the empire and Latin was imposed as the obligatory bureaucratic language. All these measures were probably attempts to coalesce a fragmented East and give it a uniform administration. Diocletian's reforms profoundly affected the structure of the Egyptian bureaucracy and brought about the gradual disappearance of most civic office in the first half of the fourth century, while new authorities were created. The municipal council or *boulê*, for instance, was replaced by a new figure, the *logistês* or *curator civitatis*, the chief executive of the city and governor of the district. All the magistrates connected with the gymnasium, the gymnasiarchs and eventually also the councillors or *bouleutai*, disappeared. It was the end of the organisational structure that Augustus had imposed on Egypt after the conquest in 30 BC.

Egypt continued to be the focus of anti-imperial revolts and its capital Alexandria remained the theatre of the election of new Roman emperors. In 297, a certain L. Domitius Domitianus led a revolt inspired by fiscal and social oppression; he was declared emperor and controlled the country for approximately a year, until Diocletian personally quelled the revolt. According to a legendary tradition, Diocletian vowed to slaughter the Alexandrian population until the rivers of blood reached the knees of his horse, but the horse stumbled as Diocletian entered the city, and the Alexandrians dedicated a statue of the animal to thank it for saving them. Some proceedings of the city council of Oxyrhynchus that mention the visit of an emperor, accompanied by the prefect, after May 298, probably refer to Diocletian, who was sailing up the Nile after his victory over Domitianus. At about this time, further documents show that complex preparations and expensive arrangements were made for an imperial visit to the city of Panopolis and the southern frontier, where the emperor fought the nomadic tribe of the Nobades. This battle, however, resulted in defeat for Rome, and the frontier was withdrawn up to the island of Philae at the First Cataract.

A papyrus document (*PCairIsid* 1) preserves an edict of 16 March 297 in which the prefect Aristius Optatus clarified the duties of the Egyptian populations towards the empire: 'For it is fitting that each person discharge with the utmost enthusiasm everything that is due to their loyalty, and, if anyone should be seen doing otherwise after such concessions, he will risk punishment ... The collectors of every kind of tax are also reminded to be on their guard, with all their strength, for, if anyone should be seen transgressing, he will risk his head.' Tax collectors no longer simply risked a fine, as in previous centuries, but could be sentenced to death for failing in their duties. Diocletian probably wanted to establish a firmer grip on the finances of the country, however his measures did not resolve the crisis.

In the meantime another transformation was taking place in Egypt: that from Paganism to Christianity. According to tradition, it was St Mark the evangelist who brought Christianity to Alexandria in the reign of Nero. However, papyri of the New Testament suggest that Christian communities flourished in the second century AD, although it is only in the fourth century that Christianity became a mass phenomenon. Some scholars read the fourth-century decline of Greek-style institutions like the gymnasium as a development that coincided with the appearance of Christian churches and a new ideology of education and entertainment that was radically different from the classical Graeco-Roman one. Christian bishops gradually superseded pagan high priests as the administrative and spiritual leaders of local communities, and Alexandria nourished a great number of Christian scholars, mystics, heretics, and saints, as Eusebius of Caesarea tells us in his *Ecclesiastical History*. Origen, an Egyptian who wrote commentaries on the Old and New Testaments, had a large school at Alexandria which included many women students (he even castrated himself in order to avoid temptation), until he was tortured and killed in the persecution launched by Decius in 250-251. Another illustrious Egyptian Christian was St Antony, who left his home around 270 and withdrew into the Western Desert as a hermit – his *Life,* written by Athanasius of Alexandria, was a major Christian bestseller and launched monasticism throughout the Mediterranean. However, Diocletian and the other Tetrarchs initiated the most violent persecution against the Christians: a decree of Diocletian's in 303 ordered the systematic destruction of churches and sacred books and the general enslavement of Christians, and the period between 303 and 311 is known today as the 'Great Persecution' or 'the age of the Martyrs'.

As Christianity gradually supplanted Paganism as the most popular religion in the empire, the emperor Constantine and his colleague Licinius strategically issued an edict of toleration in 313 (the 'edict of Milan') that legalised the Christian religion. In 324 Constantine defeated Licinius and thereafter founded Constantinople (modern Istanbul) as the capital of his reunified empire. From this point onwards, for more than three centuries, Egypt was part of the Byzantine empire. In 324, the ecumenical Council of Nicaea also established the patriarchate of Alexandria as second only to that of Rome, with powers over both Egypt and Libya. A papyrus from Oxyrhynchus (*POxy* 3759) dated 25 October 325 is the earliest known attestation to the adoption of Sunday (the Lord's Day) as a sacred day; only a few years earlier the local city council suspended work on Thursdays, Jupiter's Day. However, Christianisation in Egypt was a slow and heterogeneous process, and traditional Egyptian religion coexisted with Christianity until at least the fifth century. Early in the fifth century Rufinus visited Oxyrhynchus and he records, perhaps exaggerating a little, that there were 12 churches, 10,000 monks and 20,000 nuns there; by the sixth century the city had at least 30 churches.

Alexandria was the home of alternative Christianities, schisms and heresies against the dogmas promoted by Constantinople. Among others there were the Gnostics (literally 'Those who Know') who saw the universe in a Neo-Platonic way, the presbyter Areios (died 336) who founded the Arian heresy that minimised the divinity of Christ, and the bishop Athanasius (bishop 328, died 373) who waged doctrinal war by arguing that both the Father and the Son were of the same substance – a view that has prevailed to the present day as Orthodox doctrine. The Egyptian desert played host to the legendary lives of the Desert Fathers, and the rise of monasticism and monasteries in Egypt deeply affected and stimulated the rest of the empire. Nevertheless, despite the triumph of Christianity, some Greek aristocrats in Egypt looked back nostalgically at Greek culture and magic continued to flourish, almost as an alternative church.

Egypt also saw some pagan martyrs, victims of Christian intolerance. In 391, when the emperor Theodosius decreed the closure of pagan temples and the prohibition of pagan cults, the Alexandrian mob, encouraged by the patriarch Theophilus, destroyed the Serapeum and possibly the library contained there. In addition, in 415 the pagan mathematician Hypatia, daughter of the philosopher Theon and the first female lecturer in Alexandria, was stoned to death in the church of the Caesareum: 'They threw her out of her carriage, dragged her to the church known as the Kaisarion and, after stripping off her clothes, killed her by (throwing) broken tiles. When they had torn her limb from limb, they brought the limbs together at a place called Kinaron and destroyed them by burning' (Socrates, *Historia Ecclesiastica* 3.10).

The Council of Chalcedon in 451 was a turning point which marked the beginning of the Monophysite schism (the belief that Christ had but one nature), and severed the Catholics from the Egyptian church, also known as 'Coptic' from the Egyptian language written in Greek letters that was becoming predominant. The schism has lasted for centuries and continues to the present day as a form of national religion. At the time it certainly contributed to Egypt's marginalisation from the rest of the empire. Although the Alexandrian patriarchs were important in the Christological disputes, Alexandria was eventually overtaken by Constantinople and also lost ground to Antioch as a regional political centre.

Fifth- and sixth-century documentary papyri mostly come from the archives of great landowning families. Worthy of mention among them is the archive of the Apions, a powerful Oxyrhynchite family with large landholdings in the Oxyrhynchite Nome and in the Fayum. The Apions were influential and had political careers both in Egypt and in Constantinople where they may even have married into the imperial family. Their estate's archive has been preserved with a huge number of documents, providing details on the management of the land and insights into everyday life. Numerous accounts record payments and charitable donations from the Apions to churches, monasteries and hospitals, and enlighten us on the links between the ecclesiastical administration and the aristocracy. The Apions also supported circus factions, in particular the faction of the Blues, illustrating the important role played by the hippodrome in sixth-century civic life (*POxy* 27.2480).

There seems to have been no general, religiously motivated opposition to the legislation of Justinian (527-565), in fact Egypt adopted Justinian's legal reforms to no lesser extent than any other province in the empire, but the country was, nevertheless, in constant turmoil. During Justinian's rule, Egypt was devastated by a terrible plague which spread throughout the eastern empire, and an earthquake also wrought havoc; the religious persecution of the Christian Copts and the growing burden of taxation further fuelled the Egyptians' conflicts with and hatred of the Byzantine court. Frequent riots afflicted Alexandria, while the southern frontier of Egypt was raided by brigands. Traditional Egyptian temples had not received state income since the third century AD and were progressively marginalised by Roman emperors; their decline reached its nadir in this period. Around 537, Justinian ordered the closure of all Egyptian temples, and the glorious temple of Isis at Elephantine (near modern-day Aswan) was shut at approximately this time. Egyptian priests became magicians and sorcerers or assimilated into the new Christian environment – the evidence of rituals and festivals show that there was no formal break between traditional Egyptian religion and Christianity. In 539 Justinian once more restructured Egypt's provinces.

The relative peace that Egypt enjoyed under the Byzantine empire was interrupted by the province's role in the *coup d'état* launched by Heraclius, the Prefect of Africa. Heraclius, who was master of Egypt, along with his general Nicetas, governor of Alexandria, planned to occupy that city and cut off the corn supplies from Constantinople during the reign of Phocas (602-10). For our understanding of the 30 years between Heraclius' accession and the Arab conquest we depend on ecclesiastical sources with a strong religious bias. In the time of the Coptic Patriarch Anastasius (died 616) and the emperor Maurice, the Sasanian Persians under king Chosroes and his general Shahrbaraz invaded Egypt and temporarily ended Byzantine rule. In 618 the keys to Alexandria were sent to Chosroes along with the spoils of war. The country was devastated by battles and famines and Alexandria was swollen with refugees who had come to Egypt after the Persian invasion of Syria. While the Persians had been relatively tolerant of the Copts, the restoration of Roman domination in Egypt in 629 was followed by ten years of persecution which, in effect, opened the way to the conquering armies of Islam. In 639, seven years after the death of Mohammed, 'Amr bin al-'As, a general of the Caliph Omar, invaded Egypt, besieged the fortress of Babylon in the Delta and subsequently conquered Alexandria. A treaty, signed by the patriarch Cyrus and 'Amr on 8 November 641, sealed the Arab conquest and the Byzantines abandoned Alexandria.

Chapter 5

Cultural and Social Issues

Fear of Egypt, and consanguineous marriage

Egypt's wealth, the abundance of its grain produce and its leading role in supplying corn to Rome and Italy made the region an indispensable and crucial area of the Roman empire. In fact, Roman emperors were well aware that anyone who controlled Egypt and its grain could easily become the new leader of the empire by cutting off provisions and starving Rome into submission. For these reasons, the whole province of Egypt was feared politically as an area that could easily turn to revolution. From Ptolemaic times, the city of Alexandria had a reputation for being unstable, which was the reason Alexandrian citizens were not allowed to have their own city council, as other Greek cities did. Fear of Egypt was a major motif in the propaganda of Augustus and served to justify and legitimise Roman aggression in Egypt and the subsequent conquest in 30 BC.

It is no surprise, therefore, that Egypt and the Egyptians had a bad reputation in imperial Rome. Tacitus (*Histories* 1.11) despised Egypt for being 'a province which is difficult to access, productive of great harvests, but given to civil strife and sudden disturbances because of the fanaticism and superstition of its inhabitants, ignorant as they are of laws and unacquainted with civil magistrates' – an accusation which is untrue, as Ptolemaic Egypt had one of the most sophisticated of all Mediterranean administrative systems, and Augustus learnt much from it. Livy (38.17.11) also displays a good dose of racism when he says that in his day the Macedonian (that is, the Greek) population in Egypt had 'degenerated' into Egyptians. From the religious point of view also, the Egyptians were regarded as barbarians for their traditional worship of animal gods – this view, obviously, did not take into consideration the fact that many Greek gods also took the form of animals. Augustus publicly despised the cult of the Apis bull and even refused to visit the tombs of the Ptolemaic kings after viewing the Mausoleum of Alexander the Great in Alexandria saying, 'I wanted to see a king, not corpses!' Finally, a chronicle of imperial history written in the fourth century, the *Historia Augusta* (*Quadriga tyrannorum*, 7-8), calls the Egyptians 'fickle, irascible, vain, offensive', and even insinuates that they had sexual intercourse with chickens.

From an anthropological point of view, there were some peculiarities which rendered the Egyptian population different and somewhat under-developed in the eyes of the Romans. The major and most discussed of these peculiarities was consanguineous marriage, that is incestuous sexual intercourse between brothers and sisters – a practice that was taboo for most of the empire's peoples and yet is well attested in Egyptian docu-ments throughout the Roman period. This topic has raised much debate among modern scholars, who have questioned how the Egyptian popula-tion could survive despite this incestuous practice, contrary to the laws of nature and of mankind. According to recent studies, it is possible that the documents mentioning marriage 'between brother and sister' do not refer to biological siblings, but rather to adoptive brothers – a family strategy widely documented in the Greek East. In other words, poor Egyptian families may have adopted a son (often from among their relatives) as a husband for their daughter in order to preserve the family line and to keep the familial patrimony undivided. It is also possible that in the official documents concerning inheritances and properties, Egyptian people lied about their family relationships, tidying them up for their own conven-ience by, for instance, declaring that their children were full siblings even if they were not.

However, when Greek and Roman writers stated that Egyptians were the only peoples in the Roman empire to practise consanguineous mar-riage, it cannot have been a complete invention. It is likely, therefore, that in some cases biological siblings did marry each other. The Ptolemaic kings are a blatant example of this practice. Ptolemy II Philadelphus, for instance, married his sister Arsinoe II and the royal couple was deified in death with the title of 'Divine Brothers', a designation which evoked the mythical wedding between the Egyptian gods (and brothers) Isis and Osiris. Subsequent Ptolemies appear to have married their full sisters or their relatives and even Cleopatra VII, the last Ptolemaic queen, married her younger brother when she was seventeen, and they became joint rulers. Thus it seems that a large proportion of the Egyptian population regarded as morally acceptable a practice that was taboo in all other Mediterranean societies. Why the Roman governors of Egypt not only closed their eyes to, but even encouraged, a practice so contrary to their own laws and morals, and why the practice actually spread in the Roman period, is still debated. A specific law permitting brother-sister marriage might have been issued by Ptolemy II himself, in order to justify his own behaviour. During the Roman period, in addition, access to the Greek class and its privileges was more strictly controlled, which encouraged endo-gamy – marriage within the family – in order to preserve the family's fiscal and social privileges. Some scholars even hypothesise that incestu-ous marriage was an important part of Egyptian identity and tradition. There is also a postcolonial explanation: a foreign, occupying force, which Rome was in Egypt, did not have any interest in improving the morals of its subjects by changing this particular custom – a country weakened by continuous incestuous marriage is easier to control.

A multicultural society?

Egypt had been a multicultural and multilingual country since the time of the Pharaohs. From the early Ptolemaic period, perhaps from after the Syrian campaigns of king Ptolemy I, foreign communities of soldiers, slaves and prisoners of war (*politeumata* in Greek) were transported to Egypt as soldiers of the Ptolemaic army and were given some land and money with which to settle. These communities included Jewish, Syrian, Idumean, Arab and other foreign soldiers and their families. They were endowed with a semi-autonomous administration, with magistrates or *archontes*, an assembly of elders or *gerousia*, a local head of the *politeuma* called a *politarchês*, and a general chief of the 'nation' or *ethnos*, called an *ethnarchês*. Each community had a temple for its national religion and was free to practise its national customs. The most populous foreign community in Egypt was the Jewish community which numbered over a million people, according to the Jewish-Alexandrian philosopher Philo (*In Flaccum* 43). Although these communities were military in origin, the documents show that foreigners performed all kind of jobs in Egypt, although they could not actively participate in the administration of the country or in politics since these areas were reserved for the Greeks.

When Julius Caesar went to Egypt in 48/47 BC to fight the last phase of his war against Pompey, the Jewish communities of Egypt supported him and indeed fought for him. To reward them he granted Jews the right to continue their ancestral religion and (most resented by the Greeks) to collect money to send to Jerusalem every year for the Jewish tax. Caesar issued a series of edicts that safeguarded these 'privileges' and served to protect Jews from the attacks of the Greeks and other neighbours in Alexandria and the cities of the Eastern Mediterranean – where Jewish communities were most populous. After the official conquest of Egypt in 30 BC, Augustus confirmed Jewish rights, but made Jews subject to the provincial poll-tax along with the Egyptians, and instituted a more rigid fiscal and legal barrier between Jews and the privileged class of Alexan-drians and Greeks. In an Augustan petition (*CPJ* 2.150) a Jew called

Helenos described himself as an 'Alexandrian', but the scribe deleted this and wrote on top: 'a Jew from Alexandria'. During the reign of the emperor Gaius (also known as Caligula), the relationship between Jews and Alexandrians worsened; on the occasion of a visit from King Agrippa of Judaea in 38 the Alexandrian Greeks attacked the Jews, burning their shops, violating their synagogues, arresting and killing many of their magistrates, and forcing all Jews to withdraw into one quarter of the city, creating history's first ghetto. Thereafter, in 39, both an Alexandrian and a Jewish delegation left Egypt and went to see Caligula in Rome. However, the emperor was assassinated in January 41 before he could respond to these delegations. Claudius responded to the Alexandrian delegations soon after his accession in a letter preserved on papyrus (*CPJ* 2.153) in which he promised that the rights of Jews would be maintained in the manner prescribed by Augustus and by the Ptolemaic kings before him, and exhorted them to be content with what they had 'in a city not their own'. He also warned Jews not to invite other Jews from overseas to Egypt, and compared the clandestine immigration of Jews to a world-wide disease. It is uncertain whether he alluded to the Jewish extremists who came to Alexandria to fight the guerrilla war against the Greeks, or to the early development of preaching that took a revolutionary, anti-Roman, or even Christian character.

The difficult relationship between Jews and Greeks in Alexandria under Caligula and Claudius is reflected and documented in an exceptionally colourful way in some interesting and enigmatic texts – the 'Acts of the Alexandrian Martyrs', *Acta Alexandrinorum* in Latin – preserved in the papyri. These are fragments of fictitious trial proceedings conducted by Alexandrian magistrates before various Roman emperors from Claudius to the Severans. In these proceedings, which pretend to be documentary reports but are actually political pamphlets, the Alexandrian magistrates exhibit their nationalistic and anti-Jewish feelings, which ultimately aimed criticism at Rome and the imperial power. In fact, these works constantly accuse the Roman emperors of granting too many privileges to the Jews and too few to the Alexandrians, who regarded their 'democratic' culture and illustrious origins as proof that they should not be subjected to an empire. In one fragment Claudius insults Isidorus, the chief of the Alexandrian gymnasium, in exceptionally violent tones (for the time) denigrating him as the son of a prostitute: 'Isidorus, you are really the son of an actress'. Isidorus, in return, accuses Claudius of being a Jew: 'I am neither a slave nor the son of an actress, but a gymnasiarch of the glorious city of Alexandria. But you are the cast-off son of the Jewess Salome!' (*CPJ* 2.156d). The constant presence in the *Acta Alex-*

andrinorum of insults and violent abuse addressed by Alexandrian magistrates to Roman emperors have made scholars doubt its authenticity. Probably, the *Acta* were a kind of 'historical fiction', or stories that were developed throughout the first two centuries of Roman rule at Alexandria (and possibly also in other cities of the Eastern Mediterranean) based on a few historical events such as the first 'pogrom' against the Jews under Caligula. These stories are important for us as they give voice to the public opinion of big cities, something that rarely emerges from either the official literature or the documents in antiquity.

The fate of the Jews of Egypt was ill-starred. After the Jewish war of 66-70 and the defeat of Jewish rebels in both Judaea and Cyrenaica (North Africa), Vespasian hijacked the 'Jewish tax' that all diaspora communities paid each year to the temple of Jerusalem and forced the Jews to pay it to a Roman financial department called the 'Jewish treasury' or *fiscus iudaicus*. Egypt's Jews, along with other communities in Cyrenaica, Mesopotamia and Syria, organised a major revolt under the emperor Trajan (the so-called 'Diaspora Revolt') but were crushed by the Roman legions under the command of Trajan himself and his successor, Hadrian. In Egypt, Jewish *politeumata* were virtually annihilated after this time and the emerging communities of Christians became Rome's new enemy and the object of Roman emperors' persecutions. While it seems that Hadrian was quite tolerant towards Christians, major persecutions took place under Marcus Aurelius, the Severans and, above all, Decius in 250-1 and Diocletian until Constantine's edict of religious tolerance issued in 313.

To what extent a society is cosmopolitan can also be judged by its language. Language, so it appears, was not regarded as a problem; across the empire most provincials used languages other than Latin. This was probably the key to the success of Roman administration as, despite the mosaic of languages and cultures in the provinces, all official written communications were either in Latin (in the western provinces) or Greek (in the eastern part of the empire). Bilingualism rapidly spread, as the class of public officials often needed to both speak the local language and write in either Latin or Greek. In Roman Egypt the imperial administration never managed to impose Latin, and Greek remained the language of bureaucracy and administration until the Arab conquest. The Egyptian language, however, declined after the Roman conquest as Augustus ordered that all official contracts and acts be submitted in Greek. It was, naturally, native Egyptians who had to learn the language of the occupiers; the Roman 'immigrant' high officials were under no obligation to learn the language of their hosts. Traditional Egyptian temples, where people went to have their documents written by professional scribes, were replaced by the Greek *grapheion*, or office, of the *stratêgos* or regional governor; Demotic, the cursive script derived from Egyptian hieroglyphs that was the standard documentary script in the Persian and Ptolemaic periods, gradually declined. By the second century AD Demotic is docu- mented only in tax receipts (mostly from the Thebaid in the south of Egypt) and for temple purposes. All Egyptian speakers had to write their documents in Greek and for most – apart from priests – there was no need to learn the difficult Demotic script. The situation changed in the Christian period when a new Egyptian language developed written in Greek char- acters with the addition of a few signs: this was the origin of Coptic. The old hieroglyphs and Demotic scripts died out after the decline of paganism and the destruction of all pagan temples, and the last Demotic writings are found in some fifth-century AD graffiti from the Egyptian temple of Philae in the far south of Egypt.

Education and schools
The recent archaeological discovery of lecture rooms at the Alexandrian archaeological area of Kom-el-Dikka has cast new light on the organisa- tion of teaching and schooling in Roman Egypt. The country has supplied an immense body of papyri on which are preserved school exercises and school texts throughout the Roman period, and which greatly contribute to our understanding of what it meant to go to school or university in a Roman province. There were three main levels of schooling in the Greco-Roman world: primary school for reading and writing, grammati- cal education, that is the study of the poets and literature, and rhetorical education. This type of education was particularly useful in order to pursue a career in politics or law, as rhetorical training prepared students to give speeches in law courts and assemblies equipping them for any job in public administration. It is likely, in addition, that in Rome and big cities such as Alexandria or Antioch, there were two main tracks or curricula that were determined by the social provenance of the alumni. While lower-class students learnt basic literacy in primary schools and then left school, the privileged acquired the rudiments either at home or at school from a private teacher and went on to 'liberal schools', so-called because they provided an education reserved for free-born children.

The Greek gymnasium was a centre of education as well as athletic and military training for the Greek élites. Roman emperors were always eager to promote the higher education of local élites, since these formed the leading class of the provinces, and many gymnasia were built in the district capitals as early as the Augustan period. At Oxyrhynchus, as well as in many other Egyptian cities, the gymnasium was close to the baths and hosted sports and other intellectual activities, including lectures, though we cannot be certain that the gymnasium hosted schools and students on a regular basis. We actually have little archaeological evidence of schools and lecture rooms, but this ought not be taken as evidence that there were no schools. As a matter of fact, recent studies have shown that in Roman Egypt – as is the case with other modern and pre-industrialised Mediterranean countries – schooling and teaching often took place in informal contexts, such as the private houses of either the teacher or the student or in open-air settings like gardens, porticoes and squares. Parents had a duty to sponsor their children's education and constantly appear in the papyri as the source of student funding.

The evidence from Egypt confirms the theory that the actual contents of education, the curricula and subjects taught, were pretty uniform and standardised throughout the Roman empire. Basic grammar and writing exercises, syllabaries, lists of words and other short texts from primary schools have come down to us on a great number of papyrus rolls – a sign, perhaps, that elementary school was the most widespread form of education and levels of attendance were fairly high. At primary school students had to learn reading and writing and some basic arithmetic in order to enter any profession. Unfortunately, no evidence of specific schools at a secondary level has survived so far, except one document (*POxy* 3.471) which talks of *didaskaleia* – literally, 'teaching spaces' devoted to the instruction of young men, places worth spending the day. In secondary schools, however, students learnt to read more fluently and devoted more time to the main texts studied: Euripides and Homer, with the *Iliad* at the centre of the grammatical curriculum, and Demosthenes (especially the *Philippic Orations* and the *De Corona*) as the fulcrum of rhetorical training. From late antiquity learning took place in the form of long lists of questions and answers (the so-called *erotêmata*), a kind of catechism that covered all fields of education and systematised materials that students had to learn by heart. An Oxyrhynchus papyrus (*PSI* 1.85) has preserved a fragment of one of these 'rhetorical catechisms', while several other rolls show examples of grammatical handbooks called *Technai* ('Arts'), complete with lists of declensions, conjugations and exercises.

Naturally, Alexandria was a powerful draw on upper-class boys, who often moved there to study. An interesting letter on papyrus (*POxy* 1.119) records a young boy, Theon, begging his father to send him from Oxyrhynchus to Alexandria to study, while another father is worried about the bad company and distractions that may attend his two boys in Alexandria – the 'tentacular cosmopolis' of the time – and asks some acquaintances to keep an eye on them. Women seem also to have been involved with education, both as students' mothers and as teachers. Perhaps female tutors in primary schools were regarded as more suitable for girls, though we cannot be certain about this. A papyrus from Oxyrhynchus (*POxy* 31.2595) records a female primary school teacher in the third century, while in another document (*POxy* 50.3555) a young slave-girl, Peina, is raised by a woman who provides for her as a mother and who even pays for a female tutor to give singing lessons to the child. The major problem with carrying out work on female education is our lack of precise knowledge of the curriculum for women's studies. It is likely that music played a role, and also that the tutors were different to those who taught boys.

Women's voices
A recent collection of women's letters from Egypt from the period 300 BC to AD 800 constitutes an invaluable source on the lives and voices of women in Ptolemaic and Roman Egypt. These documents are among the most sincere testimonies of ordinary, real women, texts that allow us to hear women's voices, ideas, thoughts and preoccupations over two millennia after they lived. Since most women were illiterate, wealthy ladies often dictated letters to a secretary or a slave. It is impossible to distinguish in the Greek papyri distinctly 'female' handwriting, and it is also difficult to tell to what extent women were literate. All we can say venture at the moment is that literacy may have been more widespread than scholars have assumed. An Augustan archive of four letters written in 28 BC (*BGU* 4.1204-1207) shows a certain Isidora writing business communications full of instructions and injunctions to her 'brother' Asklepiades ('brother' is an term of endearment widely used in letters that does not imply real kinship ties). It is likely that at least two of the letters were written by Isidora herself in a hasty script and less-than-perfect Greek. She probably did not read and correct her own letters, though the letters that she dictated are more polished and stylish.

Other papyrus documents illustrate the reactions of Egyptian women to wars and revolts. An archive of documents from Hermopolis preserves a lively account of the Jewish revolt of 115-117. In the letters addressed to the *stratêgos* of the Apollonopolite Nome (Heptakomias), Apollonios, from his mother Eudaimonis and his wife Aline we can clearly hear the women's voices. They wrote the correspondence personally since the men were all away from Hermopolis in the war. Eudaimonis, whose writing displays a good knowledge of Greek grammar and spelling, complains that she cannot find help for the weaving because of the scarcity of labour during the war and talks about the damage to the fields and villages, the consequences for trade, and the lack of food supplies (*CPJ* 2.438.1-6).

The documents show that the women's main activity was to supervise the weaving, together with servants and slaves. In another document from the same archive (*PGiss* 19), Aline, worried for her husband who had just left for the war, claims that 'neither drink nor food do I approach with pleasure, but staying awake continually night and day, I have a single anxiety, about your safety'. The family belonged to the Hellenised upper class, and there is no doubt that most of the correspondents, including the women, could quite confidently write at least the letters' closing greetings, though the main body of the texts was written by servants.

Generally, Roman letters written by women display a simple, practical style characterised by brevity and efficiency. Letters were, for them, the equivalent of talking, and therefore present brief and informal messages which use a few only stereotyped epistolary formulas. During the fourth century letter writing became more complicated, as a more formal and artificial style was required, and the writing of letters was thus entrusted to specialists of this new 'Byzantine' style. It is probable that, after this point, women who had no access to a professional scribe refrained from sending letters. Letters written in Coptic, by contrast, reverted to a more colloquial style and a simplicity which the Greek language had lost permanently. Most of the Coptic letters are religious in content (many contain prayers) and are addressed to clergymen. Again, our letters do not tell us clearly whether women scribes were present in Christian monasteries, although, as we noted in the section above, there is evidence that wealthy households in Roman Egypt may have had female teachers and secretaries.

The role of women in Egypt is an important one. The Greek settlers who colonised Egypt in the Ptolemaic period found that Egyptian women had enjoyed a higher degree of independence and freedom than Greek ones since at least the sixth century BC. They married only when they chose, and marriage did not require any ceremony or documentation but was declared on the basis of cohabitation. In addition, they were able to terminate marriage unilaterally and retained their full rights to their own property. They also engaged in business transactions such as money-lending, and could sell property and sign contracts without any need for approval from a husband or male supervisor. The Greek conquest dictated that women should always have a male guardian (*kyrios*, 'lord') who represented them and signed on their behalf in legal transactions, and the Roman domination imposed further limits on the freedom of female Roman citizens in Egypt. These women became subject to the perpetual guardianship (in Latin *tutela*) of male kinsmen and had no legal independence unless they had three children (the 'right of the three children' introduced by Augustus). Although it is difficult to assess the real impact of the Roman conquest on the rights of Egyptian women (most of whom did not, in fact, have Roman citizenship), the papyri suggest that throughout the Roman period upper-class women in Egypt retained a higher degree of independence than in other areas of the Mediterranean.

Chapter 6

Alexandria

Alexandria was founded by Alexander the Great on 7 April 331 BC on a site called Rhakotis (literally, 'construction site') near the Delta of the Nile and two magnificent natural harbours, the Great Harbour to the east and the *Eunostos*, 'Harbour of Fortunate Return', to the west. It was carefully planned by Alexander and his architect Deinokrates of Rhodes, and was organised according to the principles of Greek architecture with a rectilinear grid of streets punctuated by Greek-style buildings. It had five quarters named after the first five letters of the Greek alphabet, *Alpha*, *Bêta*, *Gamma*, *Delta* and *Epsilon*; in the early Roman period, two of them (*Bêta* and *Delta*) were mostly occupied by a community of Jews who had lived there from the times of the first Ptolemaic kings. By 320 BC Alexandria had replaced Memphis (modern Cairo) as the new capital of Ptolemaic Egypt with the privileged and autonomous status of *polis* (city-state) and remained the most cosmopolitan and beautiful Mediterranean city throughout the Ptolemaic and Roman periods. In Roman times it was called *Alexandria ad Aegyptum* – 'by Egypt' – as a typically Greek city, culturally closer to Athens than to the Egyptian countryside. Given its high level of development and its population of about 500,000 inhabitants, Alexandria was often considered a possible alternative capital of the Roman empire. However, in the late antique period, Constantine's foundation of Constantinople (Istanbul) supplanted both Rome and Alexandria as the centre of the empire.

Alexandria's topography was unique, as its two main harbours were divided by a dyke called Heptastadion – 'seven *stadia*' from the Greek measure of length (1 *stadion* = c. 175 metres) – which linked the mainland to the Island of Pharos. Here stood a lighthouse that had been built in the third century BC by the architect Sostratos of Knidos, regarded as one of the seven wonders of the world. It consisted of four storeys: the ground floor was square, the second octagonal, the third circular and the fourth contained a fire; the image of the flames was projected out to the sea through a complex system of mirrors to direct approaching sailors. By the time of the Arab conquest the Pharos had been severely damaged and in modern times most of the island has sunk (other than a site called Fort

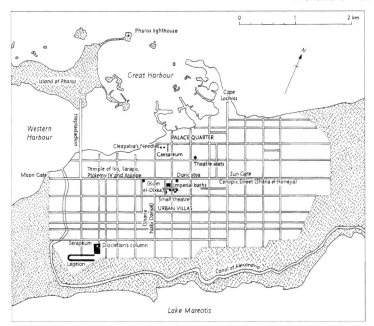

Fig. 3. Reconstructed plan of Roman Alexandria (after J. McKenzie, 'Glimpsing Alexandria from Archaeological Evidence', *Journal of Roman Archaeology* 16/1 (2003), 42-3).

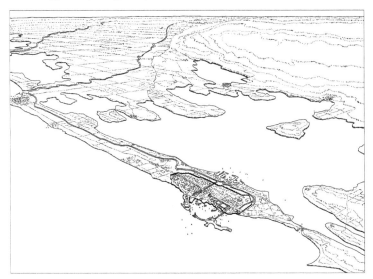

Fig. 4. View of ancient Alexandria, between the Mediterranean and Lake Mareotis.

Fig. 5. Reconstructed view of the island of Pharos, and the lighthouse.

Qait-Bey) and is the object of underwater excavations. To the south of the city lay the immense Lake Mareotis, which had an important port on its southern shore and was linked to the Nile by a network of canals. Alexandria was thus in a strategic position between the Nile Valley and the Mediterranean, a position that facilitated the transport and exportation of grain from Egypt to both Alexandria and Rome. From the Nile valley, in addition, further caravan routes linked Egypt with the Red Sea ports and the Far East. We know that trade in luxury goods and spices with India and Arabia existed from the Ptolemaic period, and that the Roman emperors greatly increased it.

In the twenties BC, the geographer Strabo from Amasia in Cappadocia accompanied the prefect of Egypt, Aelius Gallus, to Alexandria as part of an exploratory tour of Egypt. His description of the city and the country in Book 17 of his *Geography* remains one of the most accurate and vivid 'guides' available. Strabo describes the harbour and the neighbouring

Fig. 6. Reconstruction of the Pharos lighthouse.

buildings: the theatre; the temple of Poseidon; the Caesareum or Kaisareion, the temple built by Cleopatra to Julius Caesar; the emporium or
market square; the warehouses storing the grain for export, and the
ship-houses. Then he goes on to describe the two main arteries of
Alexandria as gigantic streets some 30 metres wide; the Necropolis or
Greek cemetery; the grandiose sanctuary of Serapis, the Serapeum; the
amphitheatre; the stadium and the gymnasium complex that included a
racing area, baths, porticoes more than a stadium in length, and gardens.
The royal palace was another immense complex that, according to Strabo,
covered more than one third of the city as every Ptolemaic king had added
some new buildings to the existing ones. The Jewish philosopher Philo,

who lived in Alexandria at the time of the emperors Augustus, Tiberius and Caligula, describes in detail the Kaisareion, which was probably completed and renamed *Sebasteion* or 'temple of Augustus' after 30 BC. This temple, he says, was 'decorated on an unparalleled scale ... surrounded by a girdle of pictures and statues in silver and gold, forming a precinct of enormous breadth, embellished with porticoes, libraries, chambers, groves, gateways, broadwalks and courts'. Members of the Napoleonic expedition of 1798 could still see some remains of the Caesareum, which have now disappeared. They saw, for instance, the two huge obelisks from the time of Thutmosis III which Augustus placed in front of this temple in 13 BC, and which in modern times were renamed 'Cleopatra's needles'. The obelisks were donated by Egypt to Britain and the USA, and are located respectively on the Victoria Embankment in London and in Central Park, New York.

Another major tourist attraction of Alexandria was the tomb of Alexander the Great, also known as *Sôma* ('the Body' in Greek) or *Sêma* ('the Tomb'), possibly located near the Mausoleum of the Ptolemaic kings. Here the mummified body of the great conqueror was kept in a glass coffin and was visible to tourists. Unfortunately the site is not visible today, indeed the search for the tomb of Alexander has become an almost epic enterprise as several archaeologists have struggled to identify its possible location. A massive alabaster tomb that was the entrance to a larger *hypogeum* in the Latin cemeteries exhibits Macedonian-style decoration and could be, according to a hypothesis formulated by the archaeologist Adriani in the 1960s, the tomb of Alexander or of a Ptolemaic dignitary.

The Serapeum or temple of Serapis was one of the most important religious and cultural centres of the Mediterranean. It was Ptolemaic in origin, since Ptolemy I had actually invented the new Hellenised god Serapis from a fusion of the Egyptian Gods Osiris and the Apis Bull. The new god became the patron deity of Alexandria and the protector of the Ptolemaic dynasty, and served to strengthen the links between Macedonian rulers and the traditional religion of their Egyptian subjects. The Ptolemaic Serapeum was built on a key point in Alexandria, a high plateau or acropolis visible from the sea. The Serapeum was restructured during the Roman period and remained an immensely important sanctuary. The recent excavation of the site has brought to light a huge courtyard with lecture rooms, smaller shrines and a portico that contained a small library holding religious texts including the Hebrew Bible and its Greek translation, the Septuagint. In the middle of the courtyard stood the huge main temple where there was a famous chryselephantine ('gold-and-ivory') statue of the god Serapis made by the Athenian sculptor Bryaxis. The

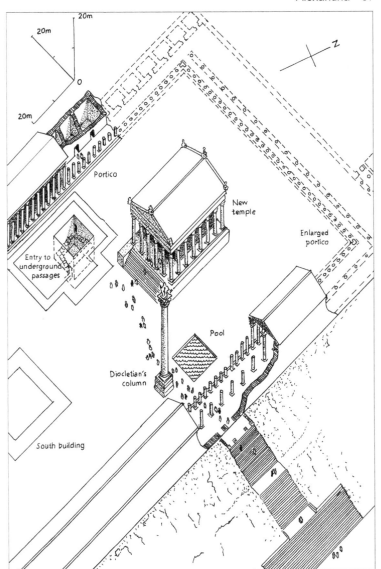

Fig. 7. The Serapeum.

temple was rebuilt after a fire destroyed part of it in 181 and it remained an important shrine for Greeks, Egyptians, and probably also Jews and Christians, until it was destroyed in 391 on the orders of the Christian patriarch Theophilus after emperor Theodosius II had decreed the closure

Fig. 8. Bust of Serapis.

of all pagan temples throughout the empire. Nowadays the most evident archaeological remnant that can be seen on the site of the Serapeum is the so-called 'Pompey's Pillar', a giant monolithic granite column which was erected by the prefect Publius – not for Pompey, as was erroneously believed, but for Diocletian after the emperor had defeated the usurper Domitius Domitianus around 298. The column was originally topped with a colossal porphyry statue of the emperor, as a fifth-century mosaic from Sepphoris (Israel) representing Alexandria shows clearly. In the nineteenth century it was fashionable for upper-class Europeans to climb the column and even have picnics at the top!

The major cultural institutions of Alexandria were the Museum (from the Greek *Mouseion*, 'Shrine of the Muses') and the two Libraries, one in the Museum and a smaller one in the Serapeum. The Museum was founded by Ptolemy I Soter and was probably finished by his son Ptolemy II Philadelphus in the Royal quarter near the palace as a temple to the

Fig. 9. Diocletian's Column (also known as 'Pompey's Pillar').

Muses and an intellectual centre. It rapidly became the focus for a lively international community of scholars and academics in various fields, from medicine and literature to mathematics, astronomy and geography. This institution offered scholars a revenue and communal meals so that they could engage freely in their studies. It was presided over by a priest nominated by the Ptolemies and, subsequently, by the Roman emperors, whose task was to administer the collective revenues of the Museum. Although intellectual circles met around temples of the Muses in the Greek classical world as well, the Alexandrian Museum, modelled on the example of the Athenian Lyceum, was the first state-funded scholarly community of antiquity and remained the most important cultural centre of the Mediterranean until the third century, when emperors like Severus and Diocletian gradually dismantled it. The destruction of the Museum marked the beginning of the decline of Alexandria as the cultural centre of the Mediterranean.

The Library stood adjacent to the Museum, and was one of the most renowned of the ancient world. Founded by the early Ptolemies, it contained probably 50,000 to 60,000 books (not 500,000, as some ancient sources exaggerated). According to tradition, from Ptolemaic times every ship that arrived in Alexandria was obliged to hand over all books on board for copying. Many famous scholars worked in the Alexandrian library, from the geographer Eratosthenes, who successfully measured the earth's meridian, to the poet Callimachus of Cyrene, and Galen of Pergamum, the head of an important medical school in the second century AD. Alexandria was also the centre of a Platonist and Aristotelian philosophical school, which directly influenced the rise of Christianity in Egypt as a religion intertwined with Neoplatonist thought. The library caught fire on various occasions in antiquity, apparently for the first time in 48/47 BC when Julius Caesar attacked the forces of Ptolemy XIII to defend Cleopatra. However, contrary to an ancient belief, only some warehouses storing books near the harbour were destroyed on that occasion, and not the actual library. The major fire that destroyed most of the library probably took place in AD 272, when the emperor Aurelian recovered Alexandria from the Palmyrene invasion. Some of the books housed in Alexandria, such as Aristotle's works, survived and were actually salvaged by the Arab conquerors, who passed them down to us in Arabic.

Underwater excavations led by two major teams, one French and one American, at the *Centre d'Études Alexandrines* (*CEA*) have unearthed an immense wealth of archaeological remains that stood under the waters of Alexandria's harbour. They have, for instance, discovered that the Heptastadion was integrated into the ancient street grid, and was not at an angle as earlier reconstructions imagined it. They also found many statues, including an Isis figure, a number of sphinxes and many fragments of architectural decoration, perhaps belonging to palaces built by the shore. A systematic exploration of the harbour areas which lay near the Royal Palace Quarter has brought to light the remains of a palace which archaeologists claim was that of queen Cleopatra – although this identification has not been proved. Other less spectacular but equally important finds have been those of around forty shipwrecks (that is, wrecks of ancient ships along with their cargoes) of which two, one Rhodian from the third century BC and one Italian from the first century BC, have been fully studied, yielding information that helps economic historians to reconstruct the size and organisation of ancient cargoes.

The other most important and extensive archaeological site at Alexandria is in the area called Kom el-Dikka, where Polish archaeologists began digging in the 1960s and continue to the present day. In the early Roman period this area contained luxurious Greek-style homes, but by the mid-fourth century AD these residences had been abandoned, the whole area reorganised and new public buildings constructed. It is thus mainly a late Roman and Byzantine site. There is a gymnasium, a small theatre or *odeion*, a bath complex and a series of 'lecture rooms' or *auditoria*, which, as has been said above, may have been part of a larger school or educational institution. The bath complex was built of brick in the fourth century over a huge area of three square kilometres, and remained in use until the seventh century. Water for the baths was supplied by a large cistern (36 by 40 metres) complete with several chambers – cisterns were a typical feature of the Alexandrian hydraulic system, and one that the Arab conquerors took over from the late antique period. The three lecture rooms date from the early sixth century. Two lecture rooms are horse-shoe-shaped and have seats in tiers and a seat in the middle, the third is square-ended, and another ten similar rooms and other buildings including a latrine and private houses with baths have been recently found in their vicinity. The site of Kom el-Dikka has also yielded a Roman theatre, the semicircular so-called 'small theatre', built some time between the fourth and seventh centuries. It has been suggested that this was used as a *bouleutêrion*, that is for the meetings of the city council, as well as for entertainment. At its top there is a row of unmatched reused columns, and it is likely that the theatre originally had a domed roof. The building opened to a west portico with a granite colonnade and limestone floor. Inscriptions carved on its seats in the later period carry evidence of the circus factions of Alexandria. Among other finds there are also many houses and workshops dating from the fourth to the mid-seventh century. Often these houses are clustered in blocks of eight with a larger adjoined house with a peristyle court and a pool. In the largest of these houses we can see a large corridor with a line of workshops, at the end of which there is a latrine (all houses had a proper sewage system) and a staircase – a sign perhaps that the private homes of the workshops' owners were on the (now lost) upper floor. There are also remains of geometric mosaic flooring and paintings, including the remains of a painting depicting the Virgin and Child accompanied by an Archangel.

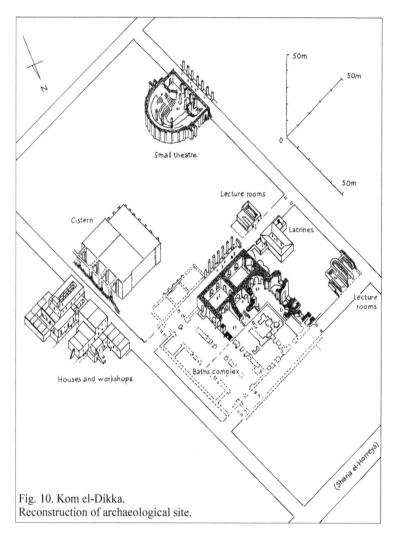

Fig. 10. Kom el-Dikka.
Reconstruction of archaeological site.

Chapter 7

Oxyrhynchus

A 'waste-paper city'

Bernard Pyne Grenfell and Arthur Surridge Hunt, two students at Queen's College, Oxford, took advantage of the British colonial presence in Egypt to begin the excavation of a little town in middle Egypt in 1895: el-Behnesa on the river Bahr-Yusuf ('Joseph's Canal') in Arabic or, in the Greek documents, Oxyrhynchus, the 'City of the Sharp-Nosed Fish', from the sacred animal worshipped there. Their sponsor was the Egypt Exploration Fund (now the Egypt Exploration Society). The once flourishing town had shrunk to a couple of mosques, some Arab tombs and some houses close to the canal. The ancient city was a wasteland of rubbish heaps and sand – the rubbish mounds were ancient, and in one case the excavators recovered papyrus rolls inside the basket in which they had been thrown away. Grenfell and Hunt hired over 100 Egyptian *fellahin*, men and children, to dig trenches ten metres deep in the rubbish mounds to the damp base level of the mounds. Hunt sorted and packed the finds and took beautiful photographs while Grenfell supervised the workmen. The six excavation seasons between spring 1903 and 1907 yielded over half a million fragments of papyrus, about 700 boxes full; these were shipped to Oxford, where they were opened and cleaned and where they are still – between the pages of the *Oxford University Gazette* in the Papyrology Rooms of the Ashmolean Museum (now the Sackler Library). Meanwhile, the inhabitants of Oxyrhynchus dug up the site in search of the precious ancient detritus or *sebakh* that was used as fertiliser. These excavations yielded numerous papyri, which were sold on the antiquities market. After Grenfell and Hunt left, the digs were taken over by the Italian *Società per la ricerca dei papiri* from 1910 to 1914, and then by a new Italian expedition under the guidance of Evaristo Breccia that ran from 1927 throughout the 1930s.

The ruins found in the excavations, together with the descriptions found in the documents, help to reconstruct the ancient city of Oxyrhynchus. It was a walled city with at least five gates, with a theatre that could host eight to twelve thousand spectators. It had great colonnaded streets like those found at Antinoupolis, a gymnasium, baths and *stoai* (porticoes). Its streets were named after their inhabitants – Cretans, Jews – or

Fig. 11. Oxyrhynchus
('sharp-nosed') fish.

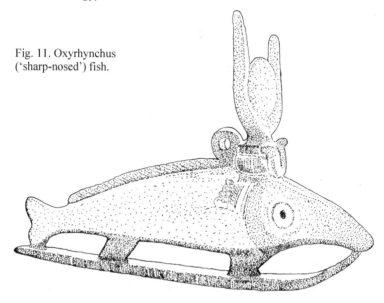

after trades – the Gooseherds, the Shepherds, the Cobblers' Market – while other neighbourhoods took their names from public buildings, temples or military barracks, such as the *kampos* (military camp) and the Troopers' Fodder Store, which reflected the activity of the Roman garrison settled there, the Third Cohort of Ituraeans. The temple of Serapis, which must have been equal in size to that of Denderah, and which was often chosen as a landmark in property declarations, was the centre of business life, and many bankers kept an 'office' there between the third century BC and the fourth century AD. The documents suggest that there were about twenty Greek and traditional Egyptian temples, including those of the imperial cult, as well as two Christian churches and a Jewish synagogue. On the eastern side of the town were two quays by the canal and a nilometer, an instrument that measured the Nile flood and determined levels of agricultural productivity. Oxyrhynchus was an important *metropolis*, like Antinoupolis or Arsinoe, with a population of perhaps 20,000 inhabitants. In the second century AD the official title of the city was 'the City of the Oxyrhynchites'. In AD 202 the status of the city was below Pelusium but above Memphis in terms of access to imperial benefactions, and in 272, when it hosted the world games, the *Iso-Capitolia*, it was renamed 'the illustrious and most illustrious', replacing the earlier, single 'illustrious'. It is documented that by the sixth century there were some forty churches, each with a bishop.

The excavations at Oxyrhynchus began a new era in the study of ancient history and literature. In the first excavation, Grenfell and Hunt found a lost poem by Sappho, from a mummy mask came a collection of poems of Bacchylides, and the publication of the long-lost *Paeans* of Pindar in 1908 created a sensation in the world of scholars. The excavations also yielded whole genres of which nothing had hitherto been known, such as the *Acts of the Pagan Martyrs*, a historical fiction about the conflicts between Greeks, Jews, and Romans in Alexandria; an ancient example of a comic strip depicting the *Labours of Herakles*, and many other unique pieces, all dumped as rubbish. An endless wealth of fragments of ancient literary texts survived in this way, comparable with the traditional corpus of Greek and Latin literature which was preserved through the medieval manuscript tradition, and rediscovered in monastic libraries in the fifteenth century. Obviously the papyrus fragments date from a much earlier period, and often yield the earliest and most 'original' or 'exact' version of a text.

The Oxyrhynchus papyri also shed light on an amazingly wide range of social, economic and cultural aspects such as marriages, divorces, trials, indecent proposals, births, deaths, as well as census declarations, tax receipts, contracts of sale, leases of land and houses, school exercises, shopping lists, prayers, horoscopes and magic spells. A study of bank receipts may allow scholars to rethink the Roman economy; an edict of a governor of Egypt may hint at political reform when compared with the ancient historiography; the letter of the undergraduate student Theon to his father asking for money and lamenting the poor quality of tutorials in Alexandria sheds some light on student life in antiquity. Elsewhere, a mother had written, 'to my son Ptolemaios ... don't hesitate to write to me also about whatever you need from here ... I took care to send and enquire about your health and discover what you are reading, and he said "Book VI" and he said many favourable things about your teacher'. Another hand had written a quiz on Homer, perhaps an ancient exam-paper. A private letter on papyrus says: 'I want you to know that from the time you went away from me I have been mourning, weeping by night and grieving by day. Since we bathed together on Phaophi 12 [9 October] I never bathed or anointed myself until Hathyr 12 [8 November]. You sent me letters that could shake a stone. So much your words have moved me.' There is the soap-opera of the Oxyrhynchite weaver Tryphon and his ex-wife who assaulted her pregnant rival in the street; the love spells, the recipes for contraceptive ointments, and the evidence for brother-sister marriages – all of which cast new light on social and anthropological matters on which official literary sources are normally silent. Papyri also indicate evolution in letter writing, for instance in the style of the greeting formula which changes from: 'I pray that you are strong' and 'Keep well!' to the Byzantine: 'Your glorious brotherly learnedness should have helped my insignificance'. The City of the Sharp-Nosed Fish, in sum, exemplifies the culture of a whole empire.

Romans, Alexandrians, Greeks and Egyptians

One of the many uses of the documents from Oxyrhynchus is that they enlighten us about the relationship between Romans, Alexandrians and Greeks. The documents show the extent to which the upper classes were conscious of their privileged position. 'Please don't think me as a barbarian or an inhuman Egyptian', writes a correspondent in the third century (*POxy* 1681). The Oxyrhynchite inhabitants with access to the Greek gymnasium were limited in number, strictly controlled through a periodical *epikrisis* or 'exam for social status'. A famous registration of Greeks in the city had taken place in AD 4/5, according to the retroactive allusions which we find in numerous later documents. The Roman government buttressed this minority of Hellenised upper classes and stressed their Hellenic identity against the progressive phenomenon of integration between them and the Egyptian population. The Greeks were a source of manpower from which municipal officials could be selected for the local administration and thus they served the Roman power. It was still the case in the second half of the third century that Greek families boasted a pedigree of ten generations in order to prove their right to membership of the *ephebia*, the Greek education curriculum, the gymnasium – the cultural and recreational centre of the élite – and, in old age, the assembly of elders (*gerousia*).

Alexandrian citizens also resided in Oxyrhynchus. A certain Caius Julius Theon is described as 'high priest and chief secretary' in a land document of 7-3 BC (*POxy* 12.1434). He was granted an estate along with fiscal privileges on the land that was once that of the temple of Isis at Oxyrhynchus, perhaps as a reward for his service as high priest of the imperial cult and chief secretary of the Roman prefect in Alexandria. It is probable that the high priest C. Julius Theon was a member of the Museum too, as he can be identified as an intellectual who, according to the Suda, 'succeeded' Arius Didymus, a Stoic philosopher, as the tutor of Augustus. He was probably a member of the élite family of Oxyrhynchus who then became a member of the Alexandrian Museum, obtained Alexandrian and then Roman citizenship, and actively participated in the administration of the province. His son, also called Gaius Julius Theon, submitted a special application to the prefect Julius Aquila in order to inherit his father's land after his death, land that would otherwise have fallen to the patrimony of Augustus. The family of the Julii Theones received Roman citizenship from either Julius Caesar or Augustus, and occupied the most important offices in the city's administration, such as the post of *archidikastês* or 'chief-judge', often associated with the titles of priest, and that of *hypomnêmatographos*, 'chief-secretary', the person responsible for registers of official business. A certain Theon is documented as 'former chief-judge and chief-secretary, victor of the sacred games, exempt from taxation, priest of the Great Serapis, and priest of the imperial cult' under Hadrian. Another impressive figure is the businesswoman Calpurnia Heraklia, a wealthy landholder of the famous family of the Calpurnii, members of the Museum and Alexandrian citizens of Oxyrhynchite origins. This family owned land from the time of emperor Tiberius, which is probably when one of its members first became a Roman citizen, and held offices in the administration of Oxyrhynchus. All these documents suggest that the titles and offices held by the Theones and the Calpurnii were practically hereditary, and that a few Alexandrian families periodically competed to hold them, while always retaining close links with Oxyrhynchus.

There was a constant toing and froing between Alexandria and Oxyrhynchus, and the great landowners who moved in from the capital to visit their estates or to administer justice and negotiate revenues may have brought along the literature they were interested in. In a first-century letter, Apollonius writes to his son Apollonius who is at Alexandria: 'I have received through Herakles the boxes with the books, as you write' (*POxy* 1153). In another letter from Hadrian's time, Theon writes to an intellectual ('philosopher' in the text) called Heraklides: 'As I put all my energy into procuring books which are of service and relevant above all to conduct, so I think you should not be inattentive in reading them. To those in earnest to profit by them no ordinary benefit will accrue. What I have sent by Achillas is set out in the following list. Farewell etc.' A list of book titles headed 'written in Alexandria' follows, clearly a list of books from an Alexandrian library.

Roman citizens also owned property in the region of the town. The Roman first lady Antonia, daughter of Mark Antony and wife of Drusus (and mother of the emperor Claudius), for instance, had a large estate there which was managed by her slave Cerinthus, a man sent probably from Italy since he writes a document in Latin about her flocks of sheep (*POxy* 2.244). Other Roman landholders were mainly veterans and imperial freedmen who engaged in various business transactions and investments either on the emperor's behalf or on their own account. Among these figures is the soldier Lucius Pompeius Niger, a Roman veteran born of an Egyptian father who served in the 22nd Legion *Deiotariana* and whose papers belong to the period AD 31-62. In one document Niger complains that he has been knocked down by a donkey and has been injured. In another, he presents a birth declaration for his daughter (*POxy* 6.894), and also writes a census declaration entirely in Latin, possibly for the census of Roman citizens of AD 47/8. In another Latin letter an imperial slave, Syneros, writes to another imperial slave, Chius, about his meeting with the banker of Oxyrhynchus, the dishonesty of a certain Epaphrates, and the possibility of making much money out of a small sum. A third Latin text (*POxy* 4.737) contains a list of salaries and remunerations written in Latin with the sums calculated in Roman currency for the labourers in a textile industry at Oxyrhynchus. The names of the labourers are clearly Egyptian, while the masters are probably imperial slaves and freedmen.

The rise of Christianity

The excavations of Grenfell and Hunt at Oxyrhynchus changed the landscape of New Testament Studies, as they yielded texts that were earlier than the two hitherto earliest parchment codices, Sinaiticus and Vaticanus, both of the mid-fourth century AD. It is said that on 11 January 1897 Arthur Hunt saw the word *karphos* ('mote') on a papyrus fragment which reminded him of the 'mote' and 'beam' saying in the Gospels of Matthew (7:3-5) and Luke (6:41-2). The same roll preserved other sayings of Jesus which were only partially analogous with the canonical New Testament passages. What Grenfell and Hunt could not yet know was that these fragments were parts of the Greek version of the Coptic *Gospel of Thomas*, discovered at Nag Hammadi around 1945. Overall, among all New Testament papyri, now numbering 118, Oxyrhynchus has yielded 47. In other words, the city has yielded two-fifths of our New Testament papyri and more than half of the oldest group.

It is likely that at Oxyrhynchus Christian texts were produced to reach other parts of Christendom in a relatively speedy way, and scholars nowadays reject the previously held notion that it took a generation or longer for copies of Christian writings to reach other communities abroad. It is generally accepted that there was intense literary activity at Oxyrhynchus and that the city could have been a Christian intellectual centre or a 'Christian *scriptorium*' – that is a centre of book production – by the third century AD, as many manuscripts show corrections and alterations that seem to have been made by their original authors. There is even evidence of literary and critical scholarship at Oxyrhynchus, as the marginal notations and the critical marks that were added on the rolls show that the texts in question were scholars' copies. Early Christian texts on papyrus had a utilitarian nature; they were not destined to be precious editions for the libraries but were produced for practical, immediate use in the local churches.

Analysis of the quantity and particularities of the Christian texts from

Oxyrhynchus has raised the question whether our accepted ideas about levels of literacy among Christians, and more generally in Roman Egypt, are correct. The idea the the rate of literacy was ten to twenty per cent of the population is constantly challenged by papyrological discoveries from Oxyrhynchus, such as the document of AD 215 (*POxy* 12.1463) that mentions a literate Oxyrhynchite woman whose Alexandrian husband and his brother could not read and write, or the document (*POxy* 12.1467) of AD 263 in which a woman supports her judicial petition by boasting that 'she is able to write with the greatest ease'. One might wonder whether these are mere exceptions, or whether literate women were more numerous at Oxyrhynchus than elsewhere.

In conclusion, it is certain that Oxyrhynchus was an important Christian centre, and some papyri even state that it was nicknamed 'the Christ-loving City'. St Matthew's Gospel tells us that Mary and Joseph fled from Judaea to Egypt with the baby Jesus to escape Herod's persecution, and some traditions claim that they stopped in various cities in southern Egypt, including Oxyrhynchus. The tradition still lingers today: a little way north from the present village there still flourishes an enormous olive tree known as the 'Tree of Jesus' whose roots have been dated to the Roman period.

Fig. 12. The Goddess Isis and her son Serapis. After a Roman fresco from Karanis (Fayum).

Chapter 8

The Papyri

Egypt is by far the best documented region of the Mediterranean. Its dry sands made possible the survival of an enormous number of literary and documentary papyri over the centuries, whether they had been dumped as rubbish or glued together as cartonnage to form the wrapping or stuffing for mummies. The Egyptian papyri are a unique, fresh, reliable and generally rhetorically unbiased source which documents the history of ancient Egypt in more detail than that of any other Mediterranean area. In spite of this, the papyri have always been approached as different from other documentary sources. Deciphering ancient documents on papyrus requires a technical, advanced training which may take many years and, as as result, scholars feel that they must either specialise in papyrology and spend their time deciphering and transcribing texts, neglecting the historical context of such texts, or become classicists and historians who often do not take these kind of sources into full consideration. However, nowadays there are technical resources, for example internet and computer databases, that have been widely applied to papyrology and that may help scholars to learn to read papyri more easily. These developments help bridge the gap between papyrology, classical philology and ancient history.

From the Egyptian papyri we collect information that can be compared with what is known from the ancient historical sources, that is from authors such as Tacitus, Livy and so on; in some cases a random discovery of a papyrus has made it possible to complete or confirm the information found in the literary sources. The term 'random' is a very important one, as we must never forget that the selection of written documents which has come down to us has done so by chance. A typical example is the dearth of papyri from ancient Alexandria. As noted above, it was the dryness of the Egyptian sands that made the preservation of the papyri possible: in the area of Egypt around the Nile delta, where ancient Alexandria was sited, the land is damp and as a result we have almost no papyri from there. For this reason also we have much detailed information about what was going on in the villages of middle Egypt (the most documented area is the Arsinoite Nome, modern Fayum), but virtually nothing on Alexandria (for which we must rely on other evidence from epigraphy, archaeology and literature). We must therefore keep in mind that we have access to only a fractional part of the documents and literature that circulated in the ancient world, and the task of the historians is to try and make sense of the little we have to build up as detailed a picture as possible.

The discipline called 'papyrology' concerns the study not only of papyri, but also of inscribed tablets and *ostraka*. Inscribed tablets are wooden tablets that were covered in wax and written on with an ink reed or *calamus* like those found on the Roman site of Vindolanda, near Newcastle upon Tyne. The Greek term *ostrakon* (plural *ostraka*) indicates pieces of earthware from broken amphorae which were reused in ancient times for writing. Often, around the ancient cities (like Alexandria) broken amphorae were dumped after being used by merchants and the pieces accumulated in large heaps on the outskirts of the city. Scribes, clerks and teachers picked them up and reused them for their everyday business, so that often *ostraka* preserve ancient shopping lists, receipts, accounts, private letters and school exercises. Once used, they were discarded again as refuse, and thus have been preserved. The papyri could also be 'recycled'. Normally, a piece of papyrus roll was written on 'along the fibres' of the papyrus, on one side which in palaeography is called the 'front' or, more formally, the *recto*. On occasion a sheet of papyrus was turned over and inscribed on the back, across the fibres: this side is called by palaeographers the 'back' or *verso*. Normally, the papyrus was rolled with the written side facing in while the back of the papyrus, which was often left blank, formed the outside of the roll. A large roll (in Latin, *volumen*) was made by gluing together many sheets of papyrus. There are rolls many metres long that contain an entire literary work (for example, Homer's *Odyssey* or collected works of poetry) and rolls that are made up of different sheets each containing one or more documents. These rolls were called in antiquity *tomoi synkollêsimoi* (literally, 'glued volumes'). The word 'palimpsest' derives from the ancient practice of washing off the ink from a papyrus in order to rewrite on the same side; often the earlier layer of writing is visible underneath the subsequent writing. This practice was even more common with parchment, which was expensive and thus was often reused two or three times.

Papyrus were used to make paper all over the Mediterranean, although it was most common (and presumably less expensive) in Egypt. The abundance of papyrus may also explain the existence of a library in Alexandria. The only other place outside Egypt where papyrus was grown was Sicily (today the only papyrus grove in Sicily is on the river Ciane at Syracuse). However, papyrus was widely used in Italy. In 1752 there was a sensational discovery at Herculaneum near Naples in Italy; over 2,000 rolls of papyrus were found in the Roman villa of Lucius Calpurnius Piso Censorinus, the stepfather of Julius Caesar and a friend of the Greek Epicurean philosopher Philodemus of Gadara. The papyri had been carbonised, along with the original wooden bookshelves, in the eruption of Vesuvius in AD 79. Several devices were invented over the centuries to unroll and clean the carbonised scrolls, which contained works by the Epicurean philosopher Philodemus and by Epicurus himself, previously believed lost, and a small number of Latin papyri. After World War I there was another important discovery of Roman papyri – mostly military documents relating to the Roman army of the first and second centuries AD – at Dura Europos in Russia.

We learn from the Latin writer Pliny the Elder in his *Natural History* (13.21.70) that the Alexandrian library was in competition with that at Pergamum where books were mostly written on parchment. Parchment came to be used in Egypt only after the third century AD, but was more common in the Near East. In the 1960s some scrolls of parchment were found in jars hidden in caves at Qumran near Engedi by the Dead Sea. They preserved Biblical texts and texts from a monastic community of Jewish ascetics living in caves by the Dead Sea between 100 BC and the end of the Jewish revolt against Rome in AD 70. These scrolls became famous as the 'Dead Sea Scrolls'. An archive of papyri belonging to a Jewish family from the Hadrianic period (AD 110-132) was also found near Engedi; the documents deal with the life and business of a wealthy Jewish lady, Babatha, and are thus called the 'Babatha archive'.

From the 1800s onwards, scholars started searching for ancient documents, and began to read the papyri. The first Greek papyrus to be read and published was the *Charta Borgiana* in 1778. In 1877 a large number of papyri from all over Egypt appeared on the antiquities market in Cairo and were bought by several European countries. During their excavations on the site of Oxyrhynchus in 1895-96 and 1906-7, Grenfell and Hunt unearthed several thousand papyri from ancient rubbish mounds. These papyri have been gradually published, by Grenfell and Hunt and subsequently by other papyrologists at Oxford and London, in the series entitled *The Oxyrhynchus Papyri*, which is still being released by the Egypt Exploration Society in London. Grenfell and Hunt are famous for their excavation of Oxyrhynchus, although they found several papyri in other villages. At Tebtunis in the Fayum they discovered a cemetery of mummified crocodiles, the sacred animal of that region. After accidentally opening one of these mummies, they realised that the stuffing was made up of 'ancient scrap paper', i.e. papyri; from this discovery came the volumes called *The Tebtunis Papyri*, which include very significant texts such as the royal edicts of Ptolemaic kings. The Oxyrhynchus collection alone has so far published approximately 5,000 papyri and the collection is so rich that many thousands still remain to be read.

The language of papyri is mainly Greek. After the death of Alexander the Great, Egypt was conquered by Macedonians and became the kingdom of the Ptolemies, the descendants of Ptolemy son of Lagus who had been one of Alexander's generals. The language of government, bureaucracy and commerce was therefore Greek, though Egyptian continued to be used, especially in Egyptian temples. Documents all had to be written in Greek, and often we find papyri in which some lines appear in demotic Egyptian with a Greek translation. After the Roman conquest of Egypt in 30 BC the emperor Augustus introduced Roman law and made Egypt a province of the Roman empire governed by a Roman prefect and garrisoned by Roman legions. However, Rome did not impose the Latin language and in Egypt, as well as in the Greek-speaking Near East, Greek continued to be the official language of bureaucracy for many centuries, until (and even after) the Arab conquest in AD 641. In fact the majority of documentary papyri are Greek papyri from the Roman imperial period, especially the second century AD. Latin papyri are rarer, and mainly deal with army business. Their contribution to the study of Latin palaeography is, however, enormous.

Most papyri were found either by Egyptian farmers destroying the mud-brick houses of ancient villages in search of fertiliser, or by papyrus-hunting expeditions carried out with little or no archaeological interest. Still, it is clear that relatively few papyri were found in isolation from others. Usually they were found in collections: family papers were kept in boxes or jars, or bound together and put in window-recesses; discarded papers survived after having been thrown away; administrative documents were sometimes reused for stuffing sacred crocodiles or making papyrus cartonnage. Even the papyri on the rubbish heaps of Oxyrhynchus were often thrown away in batches, and the origin of a papyrus from a particular section may permit historians to link it with other texts. Unfortunately, however, detailed descriptions of the finds are rare and, more often than not, the connection between papyri from a single find must be painfully reconstructed by editors of the texts many years after their discovery.

Papyrology may be divided into two branches: literary papyrology and documentary papyrology. Normally, you can tell whether a papyrus is literary or documentary at a glance. Literary papyri, an expensive commodity kept by a literate élite in their libraries, are commonly written in a neat, elegant script technically termed 'book hand'. On the other hand, documents like shopping lists, accounts, contracts of sale, marriage, divorce, birth and death declarations, are usually written quickly by scribes in town offices and contain many abbreviations, numbers and symbols; they were written for bureaucratic purposes in a fixed, standard form which office clerks would be able to recognise without difficulty; the letters are linked to one another and written hastily in what is called 'cursive script', and these documents therefore seem more difficult to decipher. While literary papyri were sold to the minority of people who could read, even illiterate people had to provide documents to the government. Often documentary papyri end with two or three lines explaining that the document was written by a scribe on behalf of another person who could not write: 'I, X son of Y wrote on behalf of Z as he is illiterate'.

Literary and documentary papyri differ in their contents and purpose. Literary papyrologists study literary texts preserved on papyri and provide philological editions of such texts which may be used to improve our knowledge of classical literature. In fact, ancient literature has mainly come down to us not on papyri but through the medieval tradition, on manuscripts stored in monasteries or libraries, and the papyri often preserve the earliest occurrence of a text. If the papyrus contains, for instance, a fragment of Herodotus, the papyrologist will make a philological commentary comparing the fragment with existing versions of the passage in order to identify any variants or errors. He will try to ascertain which version of the text is the most ancient and closest to the supposed 'original' (although in the ancient world the concept of 'original text' is often a chimera). The papyri have revealed, and continue to reveal, 'new' (though ancient) literary texts and 'new' ancient authors. From the inside of a mummy mask in London, scholars at the beginning of the last century were able to read new poems by the Greek poet Bacchylides, of whom we had previously known almost nothing, and papyrologists recently published an edition of a long roll of papyrus, housed in Milan, which preserves epigrams by the Hellenistic poet Posidippus. The first excavators looking for papyri neglected documents relating to socio-economic history and concentrated on literary papyri, hoping to find something sensational like new poems by Sappho or new readings on the life of Jesus. What is remarkable is that they actually did: in the 1960s, papyri revealed the so-called apocryphal Gospels – new chronicles of the life of Jesus and Mary that differed from those previously known (in, for instance, the Gospel according to St Thomas, or the 'Sayings of Jesus' published in the first volume of the *Oxyrhynchus Papyri*).

The work of the papyrologist entails three main steps. First, the examination of an original papyrus roll and its script, often using a microscope or other technical devices such as digital imaging that may enhance the ancient scripts and show even the tiniest traces of ink. Secondly, preparation of a 'transcript', that is the transcription of the ancient script as seen on the papyrus into separate words with punctuation and accents. Ancient scribes did not divide words or use accents and punctuation, thus if we look at a papyrus we do not see separate words but a continuum which is technically called *scriptio plena* ('full writing' in Latin). The third step is the preparation of a full 'edition' which provides a translation of the text, an introduction and a commentary on the text that expands on various points. The scholar may discuss the palaeography of the text, that is the shape of the letters in the ancient script, which helps to date a document by comparing it with similar scripts of the same period.

Through palaeography one may discover the relation between two fragments that were found in different places or at different times, but were written by the same scribe or belonged to the same papyrus roll. It can be the case that a papyrus has been broken in two halves and that one half has been excavated by Germans and has ended up in Berlin, while the other half is somewhere in the British Museum, unrelated until a scholar finds them; these occurrences are increasingly frequent, as more and more photographs of papyri are made available on the internet. Through analysis of the script, a papyrologist may identify different 'hands', that is different handwriting, as well as possible errors, corrections or erasures made by the same scribe or subsequently. The text may be analysed from the point of view of the language, grammar and syntax of the text; indeed the papyri (and the Vindolanda tablets, as we have seen) have contributed much to our knowledge of the non-literary language that ordinary people used to speak about ordinary matters. If we had only Cicero, Thucydides or Greek poetry we would know very little about the vocabulary used for foodstuffs, economy, sales, law, and ancient technology, or that used in the school system.

Documentary papyri are usually divided into categories according to the type of document or contract that the papyrus preserves. Scholars use the broad distinction between public and private documents. By public or official documents, scholars mean papyri preserving laws and edicts issued by the state (that is, by Ptolemaic kings or the Roman emperors), the kind of edicts also found in inscriptions on stone. Private documents include contracts of sale and the lease of land, animals, crops, houses and other properties, as well as shopping lists, accounts, bank documents and documents relating to the life of the individual, such as birth declarations, census declarations, contracts of marriage and divorce, declarations of property and of death. A vast bulk of papyri preserves petitions, written reports addressed to the king (in the Ptolemaic period) or the provincial governor the prefect of Egypt (in the Roman period), reporting damages or an offence suffered and asking for redress or for the intervention of the police. The papyri have also preserved judicial proceedings, reports from lawsuits, while other documents concern religion and temples. There are a large amount of private letters, often the most difficult texts in terms of contents as they leave many things unsaid and provide hints, rather than explanations, of subjects. There are school exercises and, from the second century AD, we also have Christian documents, recognisable by the mention of sacred names (Christ, Mary, the Holy Spirit) and by the presence of specific Christian expressions and prayers.

In papyrology the term 'archive' is used for all documents kept together by institutions or individuals in antiquity. This includes not only public archives, for example the records of the notaries of Tebtunis or the tax records of Karanis, but also private papers such as the more than 2,000 Ptolemaic documents belonging to the archive of Zenon, manager to Apollonios, the finance minister of Ptolemy II Philadelphos. Modern historians initially consider official records, written by and for institutions (kings, government offices, monasteries, etc.) The Greeks and Romans did indeed have extensive and well-organised public records, but with a few exceptions the records themselves are now lost. We are left with copies, sometimes even originals, which were kept by private individuals who aimed at safeguarding their rights. They are often notarial documents proving ownership of immovables, contracts, letters and accounts illustrating the management of a business enterprise, drafts and copies of petitions and memoranda showing judicial procedures (naturally, from the point of view of one of the parties involved), receipts proving that a person had paid his taxes, and so on. However, officials often took home documents that were important to them and mixed them up with their private correspondence and even with their private libraries. Thus an archive may consist of private and official documents mixed together. Another archivistic principle is therefore applied differently within papyrological archives: the papyrologist does not *respect* the existing files and their original order, because this order has been lost, the papyrologist has instead to painstakingly *recreate* the original order of the files on the basis of individual texts, which were dispersed on the antiquities market.

Chronology

88-51 BC	Ptolemy XII Auletes.
51 BC	Ptolemy XII Auletes dies. Joint rule of his children Cleopatra VII and Ptolemy XIII.
48/47 BC	Alexandrine War (*Bellum Alexandrinum*). Pompey dies in Egypt. Julius Caesar in Alexandria. Love affair with Cleopatra. Ptolemy XV Caesar alias 'Caesarion' born.
47-44 BC	Cleopatra VII and Ptolemy XIV.
44-30 BC	Cleopatra VII and Ptolemy XV ('Caesarion').
44 BC	Ides of March. Assassination of Julius Caesar in Rome.
43 BC	Second Triumvirate. Mark Antony, Octavian and Lepidus. Mark Antony in charge of the East.
39 BC	Cleopatra meets Mark Antony in Tarsus. Marriage and three children.
31 BC	Battle of Actium. Octavian and his general Agrippa defeat Mark Antony and Cleopatra in Greece.
30 BC (1 Aug.)	Octavian enters Alexandria.
27 BC	Octavian renamed Augustus in Rome.
14	Death of Augustus.
14-37	Tiberius.
37-41	Gaius (Caligula).
38	Riots in Alexandria. Alexandrian Greeks attack the Jews.
39	Alexandrian and Jewish delegations to Gaius.
41-54	Claudius.
41	New riots in Alexandria. Claudius' letter to the Alexandrians.
54-68	Nero.
69	Galba, Otho, Vitellius. Vespasian proclaimed emperor in Alexandria.
69-79	Vespasian.
73	Revolt in Cyrenaica. Closure of the Jewish temple of Leontopolis in Egypt.

79-81	Titus.
81-96	Domitian.
96-98	Nerva.
98-117	Trajan.
116-118	Jewish revolt in Egypt.
117-138	Hadrian.
117 (Sept.-Oct.)	Hadrian probably in Alexandria.
129-130	Hadrian visits Egypt again. Cruise on the Nile.
130 (22 Oct.)	Antinous drowned in the Nile. Foundation of Antinoupolis or Antinoe.
138-161	Antoninus Pius.
153	Riots in Alexandria. The prefect Lucius Munatius Felix is killed.
161-180	Marcus Aurelius.
167-c.179	Plague in Egypt.
172-175	Revolt of the *Boukoloi*.
175	Avidius Cassius proclaimed emperor in Alexandria.
176	Marcus Aurelius quells revolt of Avidius Cassius.
176-180	Laws against the supporters of Cassius, possibly including some Christians
180-192	Commodus.
193-211	Septimius Severus.
200-201	Septimius Severus visits Egypt.
202	Introduction of town councils (*boulai*) in all Egyptian cities.
211-217	Caracalla.
212	*Constitutio Antoniniana* or Edict of Caracalla. Roman citizenship granted to all adult males in the empire.
215-216	Caracalla visits Egypt. Caracalla closes Alexandria's theatres and common meals at the Museum.
217-218	Macrinus.
218-222	Antoninus (Elagabalus).
222-235	Severus Alexander.
235-238	Maximinus the Thracian.
244-249	Philip the Arab.
249-251	Decius.
250-251	Persecution of Christians by Decius. Death of Origen at Alexandria.
251-253	Trebonianus Gallus.
253-260	Valerian and Gallienus.

260-268	Gallienus.
268-270	Claudius II ('the Goth').
270-272	Palmyra controls Egypt.
270-275	Aurelian.
273	Aurelian razes the Alexandrian Museum to the ground.
275-276	Tacitus.
276-282	Probus.
284-305	Diocletian.
297	Revolt of Domitius Domitianus.
298	Diocletian in Egypt to quell the revolt.
303	Decree of Diocletian orders systematic destruction of Christian churches and sacred books and a general enslavement of Christians.
303-313	Great persecution. 'Age of the Martyrs'.
306-337	Constantine I.
308-324	Licinius.
313	Edict of Milan. Christianity is tolerated.
324	Council of Nicaea.
328-373	Athanasius bishop of Alexandria.
337-340	Constantine II.
337-350	Constans II.
337-361	Constantius II.
361-363	Julian ('the Apostate').
363-364	Jovian.
364-378	Valens.
379-395	Theodosius I.
391	Destruction of the Alexandrian Serapeum by Patriarch Theophilus I, on the orders of Theodosius.
395	Roman empire divided into eastern and western halves.
395-408	Arcadius.
408-450	Theodosius II.
415	Hypatia, pagan mathematician at Alexandria, stoned to death by Christians.
450-457	Marcian.
451	Council of Chalcedon condemns Monophysites.
457-474	Leo.
474-491	Zeno.
491-518	Anastasius.
518-527	Justin I.

527-565	Justinian.
535-537	Justinian orders closure of all pagan temples. Closure of temple of Isis at Philae. Plague in Egypt.
565-578	Justin II.
578-582	Tiberius II.
582-602	Maurice.
602-610	Phocas.
610-641	Heraclius.
619-629	Sasanian Persians conquer Egypt. Keys of Alexandria sent to the Persian 'king of kings', Chosroes.
631	Byzantine rule restored.
639-642	Arab conquest.
640	'Amr ibn al-'As, general of the Caliph Omar, besieges the fortress of Babylon in the Delta. Conquest of Alexandria.
641 (8 Nov.)	Treaty signed by the Patriarch Cyrus and 'Amr.
642-750	Umayyad khalifate.
750-868	Abbasid khalifate.

Suggestions for Further Reading

The transition of Egypt from a Hellenistic kingdom into a province of the Roman empire. For a survey of Egypt's problems just before the Roman conquest see D.J. Thompson, 'Egypt 146-31 B.C.', in *The Cambridge Ancient History,* Cambridge: Cambridge University Press, 1994, vol. 9, 310-26, and A.K. Bowman's *Egypt after the Pharaohs: 332 BC–AD 642, from Alexander to the Arab Conquest* (2nd paperback edn), London: British Museum Press, 1996. For the history of Egypt under Augustus see L. Capponi, *Augustan Egypt: The Creation of a Roman Province*, London: Routledge, 2005, and now A.K. Bowman's 'Egypt in the Greco-Roman World: from Ptolemaic Kingdom to Roman Province', in H. Crawford (ed.), *Regime Change in the Ancient Near East and Egypt: From Sargon of Agade to Saddam Hussein*, Proceedings of the British Academy, vol. 136, Oxford: Oxford University Press, 2007, 165-81.

Land, agriculture and the grain supply. On the tenure of land in Roman Egypt see J.L. Rowlandson, *Landowners and Tenants in Roman Egypt: The Social Relations of Agriculture in the Oxyrhynchite Nome,* Oxford: Clarendon Press, 1996. On imperial estates see G.M. Parássoglou, *Imperial Estates in Roman Egypt*, American Studies in Papyrology 18, Amsterdam: Hakkert, 1978. On agriculture in Roman Egypt see D.D.P. Kehoe, *Management and Investment on Estates in Roman Egypt during the Early Empire*, Bonn: Habelt, 1992; A.K. Bowman and E.L. Rogan (eds), *Agriculture in Egypt: From Pharaonic to Modern Times,* Proceedings of the British Academy 96, Oxford: Oxford University Press, 1999. On the third-century estate of Appianus and its administration: D.W. Rathbone, *Economic Rationalism and Rural Society in Third-century A.D. Egypt*, Cambridge: Cambridge University Press, 1991. On a late antique family of landowners in Oxyrhynchus, see R. Mazza, *L'archivio degli Apioni: Terra, lavoro e proprietà senatoria nell'Egitto tardoantico,* Bari: Edipuglia, 2001. On the food supply see M. Sharp, *The Food Supply of Roman Egypt*, Oxford Dissertation, 1998. On granaries in Roman Egypt see G. Rickman, *Roman Granaries and Store Buildings*, Cambridge: Cambridge University Press, 1971, 298-306.

The Roman census. The evidence for an Egyptian census under Roman rule has been studied by R.S. Bagnall and B.W. Frier, *The Demography of Roman Egypt*, Cambridge: Cambridge University Press, 1994. On the Ptolemaic census see W. Clarysse and D.J. Thompson, *Counting the People in Hellenistic Egypt*, Cambridge: Cambridge University Press, 2006. On the connected problem of status and citizenship in Alexandria see D. Delia, *Alexandrian Citizenship during the Roman Principate*, Atlanta: Scholars Press, 1991. On Latin census declarations see D.W. Rathbone, 'PSI XI 1183: Record of a Roman Census Declaration of A.D. 47/48', in T. Gagos and R.S. Bagnall (eds), *Essays and Texts in Honor of J. David Thomas*, *American Studies in Papyrology* 42 (2001), 99-114.

Roman taxation. There is no recent and comprehensive study of Roman taxation, for which one should still see S. Wallace, *Taxation in Egypt from Augustus to Diocletian*, 2nd edn, Princeton: Princeton University Press, 1938. On coinage, see the section on Egypt in A. Burnett, M. Amandry and P.P. Ripollès, *Roman Provincial Coinage I (44 BC–AD 69)*, London/Paris: British Museum/Bibliothèque nationale, 1992. On land transport, C. Adams, *Land Transport in Roman Egypt: A Study of Economics and Administration in a Roman Province,* Oxford: Oxford University Press, 2007.

Provincial administration. On Roman administration see N. Lewis, *Life in Egypt under Roman Rule*, Oxford: Clarendon Press, 1983; P.A. Brunt, 'The Administrators of Roman Egypt', *Journal of Roman Studies* 65 (1975), 124-47, and his *Roman Imperial Themes*, Oxford: Clarendon Press, 1990, 215-54. For a more general overview of the administration of Egypt see A.K. Bowman, *Egypt after the Pharaohs: 332 BC-AD 642, from Alexander to the Arab Conquest* (2nd edn), London: British Museum Press, 1996, and *id.*, 'Egypt', in A.K. Bowman, E. Champlin and A.W. Lintott (eds), *The Cambridge Ancient History* (2nd edn), Cambridge: Cambridge University Press, 1996, vol. 10, 676-702. See, in addition, A.K. Bowman and D. Rathbone, 'Cities and Administration in Roman Egypt', *Journal of Roman Studies* 82 (1992), 107-27. On legal issues see N. Lewis, *On Government and Law in Roman Egypt: Collected Papers of Naphtali Lewis*, *American Studies in Papyrology* 33, Atlanta: Scholars Press, 1995. On official laws and edicts in documents see J.H. Oliver and K. Clinton, *Greek Constitutions of Early Roman Emperors from Inscriptions and Papyri*, Philadelphia: American Philosophical Society, 1989. On the Ptolemaic and Roman institution of the *idios logos*, P.R. Swarney, *The Ptolemaic and Roman Idios Logos, American Studies in Papyrology* 8, Toronto: Hakkert, 1970. On the Ptolemaic and Roman *epistratêgos*, and administration in general see J.D. Thomas, *The Epistrategos in Ptolemaic and Roman Egypt*, vol. I: *The Ptolemaic Epistrategos*, Opladen: Westdeutscher Verlag, 1975, and vol. II: *The Roman Epistrategos*, Opladen: Westdeutscher Verlag, 1982. On urbanisation, R. Alston, *The City in Roman and Byzantine Egypt*, London: Routledge, 2002. On slavery see J.A. Straus, *L'achat et la vente des esclaves dans l'Égypte romaine: contribution papyrologique à l'étude de l'esclavage dans une province orientale de l'Empire romain, Archiv für Papyrusforschung und verwandte Gebiete/Beiheft 14*, Munich: Saur, 2004. On the Jews in Egypt see J. Mélèze-Modrzejewski, *The Jews of Egypt: from Ramses II to Emperor Hadrian* (2nd end), Edinburgh: Clark, 1995.

Byzantine Egypt. See A.K. Bowman, 'Egypt', in A.K. Bowman, E. Champlin and A.W. Lintott (eds), *The Cambridge Ancient History* (2nd edn), Cambridge: Cambridge University Press, 1996, vol. 10, 676-702. For the Byzantine period, there is a new and very useful collection of studies by R.S. Bagnall (ed.), *Egypt in the Byzantine World, 300-700*, Cambridge: Cambridge University Press, 2007, which includes issues of social, political and cultural history up to the Muslim conquest. To this can be added J. Gascou, *Fiscalité et société en Egypte byzantine*, Paris: Centre d'histoire et civilization de Byzance, 2008. See also the old, but good, A.J. Butler, *The Arab Conquest of Egypt and the Last Thirty Years of the Roman Dominion*, [1902] 2nd edn, revised by P.M. Fraser, Oxford: Clarendon Press, 1978.

Bilingualism. On bilingualism see P. Fewster, 'Bilingualism in Roman Egypt', in J. Adams, M. Janse and S. Swain (eds), *Bilingualism in Ancient Society*, Oxford: Oxford University Press 2002, 220-45.

Schools and teachers. See R. Cribiore, *Writing, Teachers and Students in Roman Egypt*, Atlanta: Scholars Press, 1996, and R. Cribiore, *Gymnastics of the Mind: Greek Education in Hellenistic and Roman Egypt*, Princeton: Princeton University Press, 2001.

Women. A useful handbook on the role of women in Egypt is J.L. Rowlandson, *Women and Society in Greek and Roman Egypt: A Sourcebook*, Cambridge: Cambridge University Press, 1998. For the Ptolemaic period see S.B. Pomeroy, *Women in Hellenistic Egypt: From Alexander* *to Cleopatra*, Detroit: Wayne State University Press, 1990. On letters written by women see R.S. Bagnall and R. Cribiore, *Women's Letters from Ancient Egypt 300 BC-AD 800*, Ann Arbor: University of Michigan Press, 2006.

Religion. D. Frankfurter, *Religion in Roman Egypt*, Princeton; Princeton University Press, 1998, and on the beginning of the imperial cult, F. Herklotz, *Prinzeps und Pharao. Der Kult des Augustus in Aegypten*, Oikumene, Studien zur antiken Weltgeschichte 4, Frankfurt am Main: Verlag Antike, 2007. On the genre of the *Acta Alexandrinorum*, and the war between Greeks and Jews see A. Harker, *Loyalty and Dissidence in Roman Egypt: The Case of the Acta Alexandrinorum*, Cambridge: Cambridge University Press, 2008. On Christian texts in Egypt see R.S. Bagnall (ed.), *Early Christian Books in Egypt*, Princeton: Princeton University Press, 2009.

Alexandria. On various aspects of Alexandria in the Hellenistic period see P.M. Fraser, *Ptolemaic Alexandria* (2nd edn) Oxford: Clarendon Press, 1984. See also J.-Y. Empereur, *Alexandria Rediscovered*, G. Braziller, 1998; *id.*, *Alexandria: Past, Present and Future*, London: Thames and Hudson, 2002; J. McKenzie, 'Glimpsing Alexandria from Archaeological Evidence', *Journal of Roman Archaeology* 16/1 (2003), 35-60; *id.*, *The Architecture of Alexandria and Egypt*, New Haven and London: Yale University Press, 2007.

Antinoupolis. See the recent R. Pintaudi, *Antinoupolis*, vol. I, Florence: Istituto Papirologico G. Vitelli, 2008.

Oxyrhynchus. For a micro view of specific sites in Roman Egypt, see two recent books on Oxyrhynchus (Bahnasa): the collection of academic papers edited by A.K. Bowman, R.A. Coles, N. Gonis, D. Obbink and P.J. Parsons (eds), *Oxyrhynchus: A City and its Texts*, London: Egypt Exploration Society, 2007, and the lively overview of historical and cultural issues in P.J. Parsons, *City of the Sharp-nosed Fish*, London: Weidenfeld & Nicolson, 2007.

General archaeology. On buildings and archaeological evidence see R.S. Bagnall and D.W. Rathbone, *Egypt from Alexander to the Early Christians: An Archaeological and Historical Guide,* Los Angeles/London: Getty Publications/British Museum Press, 2004, and the excellent, sumptuously illustrated, J. McKenzie, *The Architecture of Alexandria and Egypt*, New Haven and London: Yale University Press, 2007.

Papyri and papyrology. On the application of papyrology to ancient history, see R.S. Bagnall, *Reading Papyri, Writing Ancient History*, London: Routledge, 1995, and for a more complete overview of the discipline see R.S. Bagnall (ed.), *The Oxford Handbook of Papyrology*, Oxford: Oxford University Press, 2009.

Index

CLASSICAL WORLD SERIES

Roman Frontiers in Britain
David J. Breeze

ISBN 978 1 85399 698 6

Hadrian's Wall and the Antonine Wall defined the far northern limits of the Roman Empire in Britain. Today, the spectacular remains of these great frontier works stand as mute testimony to one of the greatest empires the world has ever seen. This new accessible account, illustrated with 25 detailed photographs, maps and plans, describes the building of the Walls and reconstructs what life was like on the frontier. It places the Walls into their context both in Britain and in Europe, examining the development of Roman frontier installations over four centuries.

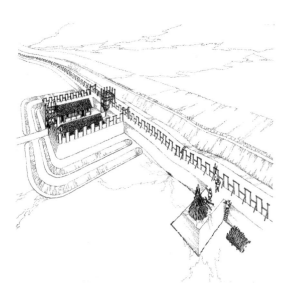

Cities of Roman Italy:
Pompeii, Herculaneum and Ostia
Guy de la Bédoyère

ISBN 978 1 85399 728 0

The ruins of Pompeii, Herculaneum, and Ostia have excited the imagination of scholars and tourists alike since early modern times. The removal of volcanic debris at Pompeii and Herculaneum, and the clearance of centuries of accumulated soil and vegetation from the ancient port city of Rome at Ostia, have provided us with the most important evidence for Roman urban life. Work goes on at all three sites to this day, and they continue to produce new surprises.

Pompeii is the subject of many accessible and useful books, but much less is available in English for the other two cities. This book is designed for students of classics and archaeology A-level or university courses who need a one-stop introduction to all three sites. Its principal focus is status and identity in Roman cities, and how these were expressed through institutions, public buildings and facilities, private houses and funerary monuments, against a backdrop of the history of the cities, their rise, their destruction, preservation and excavation.

The Plays of Aeschylus
A.F. Garvie

ISBN 978 1 85399 707 5

Aeschylus is the oldest of the three great Greek tragedians. Born probably in 525 or 524 BC, he lived through the end of tyranny at Athens and the restitution of democracy. He took part in the battle of Marathon in 490 and probably also in the battle of Salamis in 480, the subject of his *Persians*. During his life he made at least two visits to Sicily, and died there at Gela in 456 or 455.

This book deals with Aeschylus' six extant plays in the chronological order of their first production: *Persians*, the earliest Greek tragedy that has come down to us, *Seven against Thebes*, *Suppliants*, and the three plays of the *Oresteia* trilogy: *Agamemnon*, *Libation Bearers* and *Eumenides*. It also contains an essay on *Prometheus Bound*, now generally thought not to be by Aeschylus, but accepted as his in antiquity. The book is intended primarily as a readable introduction to the dramatist for A-level students of Classical Civilisation and Ancient History at school and in the first two years of university courses.

Greek Literature in the Roman Empire
Jason König

ISBN 978 1 85388 713 6

In this book Jason König offers for the first time an accessible yet comprehensive account of the multi-faceted Greek literature of the Roman Empire, focusing especially on the first three centuries AD. He covers in turn the Greek novels of this period, the satirical writing of Lucian, rhetoric, philosophy, scientific and miscellanistic writing, geography and history, biography and poetry, providing a vivid introduction to key texts with extensive quotation in translation. He also looks beyond the most commonly studied authors to reveal the full richness of this period's literature. The challenges and pleasures these texts offer to their readers have come to be newly appreciated in the classical scholarship of the last two or three decades. In addition there has been renewed interest in the role played by novelistic and rhetorical writing in the Greek culture of the Roman Empire more broadly, and in the many different ways in which these texts respond to the world around them. This volume offers a broad introduction to those exciting developments.

Early Greek Lawgivers
John David Lewis

ISBN 978 1 85399 697 9

Early Greek Lawgivers examines the men who brought laws to the early Greek city states, as an introduction both to the development of law and to basic issues in early legal practice. The lawgiver was a man of special status, who could resolve disputes without violence and bring a sense of order to his community by proposing comprehensive norms of ethical conduct. He established those norms in the form of oral or written laws. Crete, under king Minos, became an example of the ideal community for later Greeks, such as Plato. The unwritten laws of Lycurgus established the foundations of the Spartan state, in contrast with the written laws of Solon in Athens. Other lawgivers illustrate particular issues in early law; for instance, Zaleucus on the divine source of laws; Philolaus on family law; Phaleas on communism of property; and Hippodamus on civic planning.

Greek Vases: An Introduction
Elizabeth Moignard

ISBN 978 1 85399 691 7

Greek Vases is an introduction to the painted vases which were an ever-present but understated feature of life in the Greek world between the end of the Bronze Age and the rise of Rome, and, in the modern world, an important component of museum collections since the eighteenth century. The book uses specific illustrated examples to explore the archaeological use of vases as chronological indicators, the use of the various shapes, their scenes of myth and everyday life and what these tell us, the way in which we think about their makers, and how they are treated today as museum objects and archaeological evidence.

Key features of the text include a brief accessible introduction to the vases with school and university students in mind, discussion of the different approaches to vases adopted by their very different groups of users, and an approach designed to help viewers understand how to look at these fascinating objects for themselves.

Athletics in the Ancient World
Zahra Newby

ISBN 978 1 85399 688 7

The athletic competitions that took place during festivals such as that at Olympia, or within the confines of city gymnasia, were a key feature of life in ancient Greece. From the commemoration of victorious athletes in poetry or sculpture to the archaeological remains of baths, gymnasia and stadia, surviving evidence offers plentiful testimony to the importance of athletic activity in Greek culture, and its survival well into Roman times.

This book offers an introduction to the many forms that athletics took in the ancient world, and to the sources of evidence by which we can study it. As well as looking at the role of athletics in archaic and classical Greece, it also covers the less-explored periods of the Hellenistic and Roman worlds. Many different aspects of athletics are considered – not only the well-known contests of athletic festivals, but also the place of athletic training within civic education and military training, and its integration into the bathing culture of the Roman world.